Developmentally Appropriate Play

Guiding Young Children to a Higher Level

GAYE GRONLUND

Foreword by Ellen Frede, PhD

Redleaf Press®
www.redleafpress.org
800-423-8309

Published by Redleaf Press
10 Yorkton Court
St. Paul, MN 55117
www.redleafpress.org

First edition 2010
Cover design by Jim Handrigan
Interior typeset in Berkeley Oldstyle Book
    and designed by Erin Kirk New
Printed in the United States of America
17 16 15 14 13 12 11 10   1 2 3 4 5 6 7 8

Library of Congress Cataloging-in-Publication Data

Gronlund, Gaye, 1952–
    Developmentally appropriate play : guiding young children to a higher
level / Gaye Gronlund.—1st ed.
        p. cm.
    Includes bibliographical references.
    ISBN 978-1-60554-037-5 (alk. paper)
    1. Play. 2. Play groups. I. Title.
    LB1137.G73 2010
    155.41'8—dc22
                                                    2009051433

Printed on acid-free paper

To all of the preschool and
kindergarten teachers who have
continued to advocate for play as
a central and important way for
young children to learn and grow.

Contents

Foreword

If the Children Play, When Do I Teach? The False Dilemma of Developmentally Appropriate Practice

I was sitting in the square of my home town on a beautiful spring day recently, idly watching the children and families at play. I noticed two contrasting play episodes that highlighted some of the research-based lessons included in this important volume on play.

Ball Play: *Two toddlers, about eighteen months to two years, were taking turns attempting to throw a large plastic ball to each other. Of course neither could catch the ball, but they clearly enjoyed the act of throwing, running after the ball, and turn-taking. Six adults (I assume four parents and two grandparents) were standing nearby talking and watching the children. Each time one of the toddlers threw the ball, all of the adults clapped their hands, while continuing their conversations; many did not even look over at the children. Occasionally, one of the adults would exclaim, "Good throw!"*

Role Play: *My attention was diverted by a group of three older children who were involved in an elaborate role play in the bushes next to me. The oldest girl was talking animatedly to the other two and gesturing. They separated and began gathering leaves and twigs. As they were arranging the materials under the direction of the oldest, some problem arose and they began searching around. The leader pointed to some tulips and the two smaller ones scampered off to pick them. One of the mothers immediately came over to stop them from picking the flowers. She showed them the difference between dead and living plants, and after listening to them explain their dilemma, she showed them how to arrange some dead leaves to look like flowers. Their mother later explained to me that they had been incorporating a wedding story into their play, and flowers were central to the story.*

Some of the lessons these observations illustrate, that are aptly elaborated on in this volume, are obvious and some are more subtle. Clearly, children, and virtually all mammals, play because they want to and that play changes as they develop, in these two cases, from simple mastery of ball throwing and less simple turn-taking to complicated socio-dramatic play with defined roles and story lines. Less clear and something that is sometimes difficult for teachers (and parents) to grasp is that typically developing children don't need our "empty" praise to motivate them when the play is challenging and engaging. In fact, research has shown that the kind of constant "good job" praise that the parents chanted to the ball throwers could even interfere with motivation. Children who become praise junkies often won't perform without it.

What our children do need, in addition to time to play and interesting experiences and materials to enhance play, are value-added interactions. The mother in the role play provided content knowledge on dead versus living plants and information about appropriate behavior with accompanying explanations. Value-added interactions may also include a myriad of other supports such as encouragement if the task becomes very demanding, modeling new possibilities or roles, or posing more sophisticated problems for children to investigate.

Sometimes what is labeled "play" in a classroom doesn't provide children with opportunities to make choices, solve problems, work cooperatively with others, or develop rich language. What is called play may just be a short break to reward the completion of academic work or a structured learning game that only focuses on practicing skills and repeating facts. At the other extreme, play in some classrooms is viewed narrowly as a conduit for socialization, neglecting all of the other social, cognitive, and linguistic benefits of play. Here the teacher's role is mainly to manage materials and ensure children have what they need to play. In some classrooms, we even find a confused combination of both approaches, with the children playing on their own with minor assistance from the teachers (preschool's version of busy work) and the teacher pulling children out of play for "teaching time," which consists of small group or one-on-one skills based instruction or following the teacher's model for a craft activity.

Think about your work day yesterday. What would you categorize as fun, as work, and as learning? This morning I started the day finishing my thoughts about this foreword. As I reviewed some articles and wrote down some notes,

I got frustrated and kept reworking the order and wording of things. So was it work? Very definitely—hard work. Was it learning? Often, because I was refining my thinking and relearning specific aspects of the research. But the big question—Was it fun? Yes, but hard fun. I'm sure you can think of activities and tasks you completed yesterday that had aspects of work, learning, and play all intertwined, and I think this is what we mean in the field of early education when we say, "Play is the child's work."

One of the studies I reviewed investigated how children's definitions of the categories of work, learning, and play are affected by the teacher's philosophy, which in turn influences the nature of the tasks and the way the teacher frames and presents the activity. Too often, completing the task is the goal communicated to the children either intentionally or not, and the focus is on following directions and completion, not on understanding. Hermine Marshall (1994) has compared children's view of work, learning, and play in classrooms that focused on worksheets and basic skills to those of children in classrooms that focused on integrated, manipulative, and creative tasks. The children in the first viewed everything except recess as work because it was something they "had to" do. In the project-focused classrooms, children still referred to many of their activities as work, but this was because of the mental effort to understand and solve problems—the workplace of the mind rather than the factory. They were also much more likely to classify activities as learning and play. In addition, they understood what they were learning; for example, not only how to weave but what a pattern is and how to make it.

In my thirty year journey in early childhood education as a teacher educator, a researcher who has conducted classroom observations across the United States and abroad, and a state pre-K administrator, I have found that the hardest concepts for teachers to learn are how to effectively include play in the classroom and the teacher's role in play. This book remedies the problem and provides a thorough treatment of not only these issues but also the research rationale for play. Teachers who use these methods will have children who see their activities in the classroom as work, learning, and play. Teachers who read this book will be informed and prepared to defend the value of play and at the same time will be able to ensure that the play in their classrooms is valuable.

Ellen Frede, PhD
Codirector
National Institute for Early Education Research

Acknowledgments

So many friends and colleagues helped form the ideas in this book. And many contributed photographs and writing samples to the project. My heartfelt thanks to the following people:

Gail Holtz, Mary Beth Hilbourne, Mark Mason, and colleagues at Hawken School in Lyndhurst, Ohio

Joyce Kinney and the teachers and families of Renaissance Children's Center of the Colorado Coalition for the Homeless in Lakewood, Colorado

Kathy Stewart, Laurie Tischler, and the teachers and families of St. Saviour's Church Nursery School in Old Greenwich, Connecticut

Pam Knorr, Laura Hummel, Cathy Boldger, Amy Markuson, and Lisa Whitehead and the families of Walworth Early Childhood Program in Walworth, Wisconsin

Ann Allen and her fellow coaches and teachers of New Mexico's Pre-K Programs

Marlyn James of Flathead Valley Community College in Kalispell, Montana

Sue Jeffers and colleagues at University School of Milwaukee in Wisconsin

Tovah Klein of Barnard Center for Toddler Development in New York City

The staff of the National Association for the Education of Young Children (NAEYC) in Washington DC for giving me the opportunity to visit many classrooms and see play in action

Jeanne Engelmann for a wonderfully smooth editing process

Kyra Ostendorf of Redleaf Press for inviting me to write on this topic.

Introduction

> The children who thrive enter school with strong communication skills.
> They are confident and self-assured, adept at making friends, persistent,
> creative, and excited about learning. These are the qualities that children
> acquire through play. (Segal 2004, 33)

As I travel around the country working with early childhood professionals, I
hear lots of questions and misunderstandings about the best ways to facilitate
play. It seems that many teachers are puzzled as they try to figure out the best
balance between teacher-directed and child-directed activities. Some assume
that learning occurs in teacher-directed activities only—that's where academics
fit in. They see play as child-directed, free and fun, but not necessarily as a time
for learning to occur. Others think that play is an important vehicle for learning,
but are confused about how to enhance the experience for children. Instead,
they may tend to step back and see it as a totally child-directed experience and
stay uninvolved until problems arise needing their intervention. Or they may
try to inject academic skills and/or early learning standards in such a way that
the children quickly lose interest in the play scenario and become more passive
learners in the process.

As I visit preschool and kindergarten classrooms, I do not always see high-
level, mature play going on. Developmentally appropriate play is not just free
and fun. It's also complex, long-lasting, and all-engaging for the children.
This kind of play needs teacher facilitation and guidance. It takes thoughtful

planning, attention to the environment and materials, and coaching on the part of the teacher to make it happen and to sustain it. Good teachers work hard to do so.

In the third edition of *Developmentally Appropriate Practice in Early Childhood Programs Serving Children from Birth through Age 8* (DAP) released by the National Association for the Education of Young Children (NAEYC) (Copple and Bredekamp 2009), there are many statements about the value and importance of play and teachers' roles in enhancing play. Here are some of them:

- Play is an important vehicle for developing self-regulation as well as for promoting language, cognition, and social competence. (Principle 10 of the NAEYC Position Statement, 14)

- Active scaffolding of imaginative play is needed in early childhood settings if children are to develop the sustained, mature dramatic play that contributes significantly to their self-regulation and other cognitive, linguistic, social, and emotional benefits. . . . Rather than detracting from academic learning, play appears to support the abilities that underlie such learning and thus to promote school success. (15)

- A wonderful cycle of learning is driven by the pleasure in play. A child is curious; she explores and discovers. The discovery brings pleasure; the pleasure leads to repetition and practice. Practice brings mastery; mastery brings the pleasure and confidence to once again act on curiosity. All learning—emotional, social, motor, and cognitive—is accelerated and facilitated by repetition fueled by the pleasure of play. (Perry, Hogan, and Marlin 2000, in Copple and Bredekamp 2009, 50)

Throughout this book, these statements and others are used to determine the best strategies for guiding children to higher-level play experiences. As teachers become more familiar with these principles, they will be able to communicate clearly to others about the importance of play, explaining rather than defending the teaching strategies and curricular approaches that they know are best for young children. They will be able to justify inclusion of play in their curriculum rather than repeatedly explain to parents, community members, and administrators that "It's more than 'just play.'"

What Can Teachers Do?

Preschool and kindergarten teachers can be very intentional in their work to help children achieve and sustain higher levels of play. The process involves recognition of the levels of play and knowledge of strategies that enhance its depth and richness. I have seen skilled teachers who incorporate early learning standards and authentic assessment in children's play experiences without losing the joy and engagement that good quality play provides for children. It's a complex process that requires an artistry of its own!

This book analyzes that process and identifies the many actions that teachers in preschools and kindergartens can take to make play all that it can be. Many ideas and suggestions for facilitating children's engagement in high-level play are given throughout. These suggestions can be used with any of the following types of play: dramatic play, block play, play with sensory materials (sand, water), and play with manipulatives. Each chapter takes a different part of the facilitation process and looks at it in depth. Examples of play scenarios are included with descriptions of teachers' steps to enhance the play situation.

In chapter 1, the focus is on the importance of play and the key roles teachers have in guiding children's play so that it is mature and beneficial to the children. In addition, three levels of play are identified: chaotic, simplistic, and purposeful. Chapter 2 explores the ideas put forth by theorists that support the need for play and show the role higher-level play has in enriching children's learning. The differences between chaotic, simplistic, and purposeful play will be considered as well. Chapter 3 shares ways that teachers can plan for purposeful play. Teachers will provide structure and set expectations to help the play move far beyond chaotic or simplistic by carefully setting up their environments so children have interesting materials that stimulate their creativity and imaginations. Chapter 4 focuses on the ways that teachers can help children make choices so that their play experiences are positive and productive. In addition, suggestions for allowing enough time in the daily schedule for deep play to develop are given.

Chapter 5 delves into how teachers interact with children to enhance their play. It includes techniques on how to get play started, how to know when to enter and exit play, how to coach children in play, and how to use well-timed questioning. Chapter 6 focuses on the power of provocations, such as planning for field trips and special visitors, incorporating books, providing new materials, and considering groupings of children to stimulate and further deepen play experiences. In addition, the emotional nature of play is discussed. Chapter 7 gives ideas for complicating the play and taking it to even higher cognitive levels in both literacy and math by adding representation to children's play experiences. And in chapter 8, strategies for incorporating standards and goals into children's play are explored. The emphasis is on how to use observation to see standards and goals in action for assessment purposes as well as to determine next steps with the children. The relation between sustaining children's interest and engagement and adding challenging achievable goals to their play scenarios is also discussed. The conclusion provides some final thoughts.

Teachers' actions have direct effects on the quality and benefits of young children's play. I hope that this book provides a provocation to the field of early childhood education to consider the many ways that teachers can be intentional in enhancing the depth and richness of children's play. And as the guidelines in the third edition of DAP remind us

> Excellent teachers know . . . it's *both* joy *and* learning . . . they go hand in hand . . . Teachers are always more effective when they tap into this natural love of learning rather than dividing work and enjoyment. As some early childhood educators like to put it, children love nothing better than "hard fun." (Copple and Bredekamp 2009, 50)

CHAPTER 1

What's So Important about Play?

> Play encourages flexibility and creativity that may, in the future, be advantageous in unexpected situations or new environments. Some child psychologists, such as Tufts University child development expert David Elkind, agree. Play is "a way in which children learn," Elkind says, "and in the absence of play, children miss learning experiences." (Wenner 2009, 29)

Early childhood professionals have long advocated for the importance of play in preschool and kindergarten classrooms. But academic pressures, calls for accountability, and misunderstanding about how young children learn best have taken their toll, causing play to be questioned and minimized in classrooms. And many teachers are frustrated with the continual need to justify *any* time for play, let alone the long periods that children need to develop rich, imaginative, and complex play.

But good news is here! Experts from a variety of fields, including medicine, child development, psychiatry, psychology, evolutionary biology, and education, are joining with early childhood educators to communicate the vital need for children to play and the many benefits they gain from play. And they have research to support their positions. With the publication of the new, third edition of *Developmentally Appropriate Practice in Early Childhood Programs Serving Children from Birth through Age 8* (DAP) released by the National Association for the Education of Young Children (NAEYC) (Copple and Bredekamp 2009), the research of these experts is incorporated and provides teachers with a firm foundation on which to stand when explaining the importance of play to others. Hurray! Play is at the forefront of early childhood education once again.

The recommendations of NAEYC and other organizations support teachers' efforts to meet the needs of younger children by providing active learning opportunities and extended time for play each day. For example, a clinical report by the American Academy of Pediatrics states: "Play is essential to development because it contributes to the cognitive, physical, social, and emotional well-being of children and youth" (Ginsburg 2007, 182). And experts from a variety of fields agree that play is an essential component for the development of healthy children:

> Theorists . . . suggest that the *absence of play* is an obstacle to the development of healthy and creative individuals. *Psychoanalysts* believe that play is necessary for mastering emotional traumas or disturbances; *psychosocialists* believe it is necessary for ego mastery and learning to live with everyday experiences; *constructivists* believe it is necessary for cognitive growth; *maturationists* believe it is necessary for competence building and for socializing functions in all cultures of the world; and *neuroscientists* believe it is necessary for emotional and physical health, motivation, and love of learning. (Isenberg and Quisenberry 2002, 1–2)

In the new DAP, studies that support play are cited:

> A study of children from around the world, from Indonesia to Italy to Ireland (and the United States), showed that when preschool experiences at age 4 included lots of child-initiated, free-choice activities supported by a variety of equipment and materials—the kinds of environments that support play—these children had better cognitive (and language) performance at age 7 than their peers.
>
> Other research shows that pretend play strengthens cognitive capacities, including sustained attention, memory, logical reasoning, language and literacy skills, imagination, creativity, understanding of emotions, and the ability to reflect on one's own thinking, inhibit impulses, control one's behavior, and take another person's perspective . . . (Copple and Bredekamp 2009, 131–32)

In addition, the Alliance for Childhood released a passionate plea in their report *Crisis in the Kindergarten: Why Children Need to Play in School*:

> We believe that the stifling of play has dire consequences—not only for children but for the future of our nation. . . .No human being can achieve his full potential if his creativity is stunted in childhood. And no nation can thrive in the 21st century without a highly creative and innovative workforce. Nor will democracy survive without citizens who can form their own independent thoughts and act on them. (Miller and Almon 2009, 1–2)

Not Just Any Play

However, the recommendations and research do not suggest that teachers encourage just *any* play. Rather, the emphasis is on helping children to engage in purposeful, high-level, mature play, the kind of play that tells "grand stories" as in the following quote:

> The early childhood classrooms we know best are filled with the richly varied voices of the very young. Their voices collectively transform the classroom into a novel . . . a grand story in which the child characters, as speakers, have different developmental histories, varying cultural and linguistic heritages and, at any point in time, different social agendas . . . we listen for individual voices as they respond to the world around them, socially connecting, communicating, and declaring their own presence, their own importance, in the social scene. (Genishi and Dyson 2009, 32)

Preschool and kindergarten children engage in dramatic play that involves an ever-changing script and cast of characters. They build and construct with blocks or other manipulatives to represent the places in their lives. They stay with such activities for long periods of time because they are worthwhile and rewarding to them. In the new DAP, the authors cite research that shows that more complex play helps children develop a number of skills and capabilities such as self-regulation, language, vocabulary, and abstract thinking. And this

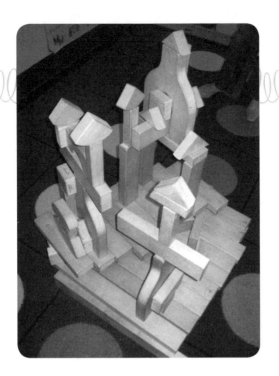

research clearly supports that these skills and capabilities have a direct connection to later academic achievement. Play is emphasized throughout the DAP guidelines as an important vehicle for learning.

Teachers Are the Key

Young children love to do things that are fun. Their enthusiasm is contagious. Many preschool and kindergarten teachers relish their jobs because of the joy in sharing that enthusiasm. However, in this age of early learning standards and accountability, teachers recognize that fun is not the *only* reason to do things with children. Teachers know children can learn so many concepts and skills that can help them make sense of their world and lead them to greater academic achievement as they get older. However, confusion reigns about where learning comes in. Is it separate from play activities? Does it happen only when a teacher is leading a small or large group? Is play something different than work? Does good, beneficial play need a teacher's involvement? If so, is it still play? These are important questions that are debated passionately within the field of early childhood education.

Teachers have an important task with preschool and kindergarten children: to provide ample time, space, materials, and support to lead the children to engage in play that is safe, socially successful, filled with purpose and meaning, and imaginative. Such play is a joy to witness. The children's eyes are bright. Their energy and engagement is high. Their voices are noisy but not overly so. They use objects for different purposes. They negotiate and compromise with each other. And they are willing to sustain the play because it is fun and rewarding. The following three interactions show teachers who recognize the importance of play for the young children in their care. These teachers realize that they have a very important job to do—to support and enhance play so it benefits the children.

Doug observes as Lucia, Marco, and Robert play "camping." Things are going well in his class of four-year-olds. Children are productively engaged in play and exploration activities. They are self-directed and attentive to what they are doing. Doug decides to sit close to the "campers" for a short time and write down the script that they are inventing. Later, he will read that script back to the children at large-group time and celebrate with them the imaginative ways they used materials and interacted with each other as they created a lengthy camping scenario. He can just see the smiles on their faces as he reads back the story of their play experience to the group.

Marissa posts some of the early learning standards from her state in the play areas of her kindergarten classroom. She uses laminated cards with specific indicators printed on them and affixes them to posters with Velcro so she can change them on a regular basis. She's found that this helps her be more goal-oriented in her observations of the children as they play, as well as in her interactions with them as she supports what they are doing. She knows it's important to follow their lead and also to recognize that many standards are being addressed as the children play at different roles, construct with blocks and manipulatives, and explore and problem solve at the sensory table.

Lorene recognizes that many of her children have not had extensive play experiences before coming to her preschool program. She can see that their play is immature, repetitive, and easily slips out of control. She has found that her involvement as a play model and coach is helpful in leading the children to more productive engagement. On a regular basis, she helps get play started. Sometimes, she acts as the patient to the children pretending to be doctors and nurses. Other times, she enjoys being served pizza and other pretend meals as they cook for her and take her orders. She's learning the signals that tell her that the children can take control of the play themselves and keep it going successfully. Then, she tries to time her exit so they can sustain the scenario on their own. But she is ever ready to step back in if necessary to help the children keep good play going.

So again the question is asked: Is play an important part of learning for a child? Play is indeed at the heart of best practices for young children. The guidelines and recommendations in the third edition of DAP identify play as an important vehicle for learning in the early years. However, as mentioned previously, not just *any* play: rather, high-level, complex play is of the most benefit to young children. In addition, teachers are to be intentional in all that they do, including planning for and facilitating children's play.

I am honored when I am invited to visit preschool and kindergarten class-rooms, and I am delighted when I see high-level play in action. I know that the teachers set up a number of conditions for that play to happen and are making constant decisions as they observe the children at play. I know that the teachers are taking steps to support the children so their play can be sustained at a high level. I also know that the children see the teachers as important partners in play. The children can trust that the teachers will be there to help them when they need it.

Recognizing Three Levels of Children's Play

Not all play is good play. Children can get hurt when they build wooden block structures and attempt to stand on them. Children can be mean and inappropriate when they exclude another child from joining a dramatic play experience. Silliness and hilarity can take over play that began in a more productive way. And repeating the same actions over and over again can show a lack of creativity and imagination. In order to make on-the-spot decisions about how best to facilitate children's play, teachers need to evaluate the quality of the play that they are seeing. In my work, I consistently see three levels of play:

1. Chaotic or out-of-control play
2. Simplistic and repetitive play
3. Purposeful, complex play that engages the children's full attention

I have seen teachers help children move beyond chaotic or simplistic play to rich, meaningful play. The children can keep this play going for long periods of time, maybe even across several days or weeks. And, in the process, the play scenarios grow more complicated. This is play that is so all-engaging that the children stand tall in confidence, using skills in a variety of ways and symbolically representing what they know and are learning about the world. This is the play that the developmental theorist, Lev Vygotsky, refers to when he says: "In play a child is always above his average age, above his daily behavior; in play it is as though he were a head taller than himself" (Vygotsky 1976, 552, in Roskos and Christie 2004, 113). The three levels of play, as well as theorists' ideas, are discussed more in chapter 2.

Skilled teachers know that their goal is to provide support and scaffolding so children reach this high level of play. If the teachers see behavior problems as children play dress-up or dig in the sand, they step in. And they pay close attention to the quality of play. If children are repeating the same actions over and over again or do not use much imagination and creativity in what they are doing, the teachers know it is time to step in with new ideas or materials.

The idea that higher-level play can enhance early childhood learning is not entirely new. The next chapter covers the educators and theorists who built part of the foundation that explains and supports the importance of higher-level play in a child's learning.

CHAPTER 2

Putting Theory into Practice

> In a four-year-old's play, we can observe higher levels of such abilities as attention, symbolizing, and problem solving than in other situations. We are actually watching the child of tomorrow. (Bodrova and Leong 2007, 133)

Chapter 1 examined why higher-level play is important. Early childhood professionals need to know the strong support they have for incorporating play experiences into their curricula and doing all they can to enhance those experiences for children. This chapter looks to define what higher-level play is, as well as what it is not. The characteristics of chaotic, simplistic, and complex play are explained so teachers can easily recognize these types of play when observing children in action. But first, it is important to understand the reasoning and ideas that support complex play. A look at the perspectives of some important child development theorists is required. Why? Because applying a theoretical framework helps teachers determine what is developmentally appropriate for the children in their programs.

A Hierarchy of Needs and Play

One way to consider the three levels of play is to think in terms of Abraham Maslow's Hierarchy of Needs. As shown in the graphic that follows, Maslow theorized that as humans function, they do so with a hierarchy of innate needs.

Maslow's Hierarchy of Needs

Some needs are more powerful than others and must be satisfied before people are able to move up to the higher levels. Thus, physiological, safety, and belonging needs must be tended to first, before energies can be focused on the higher levels of esteem and self-actualization.

In the previous chapter, three levels of play were identified:

1. Chaotic or out-of-control play
2. Simplistic and repetitive play
3. Purposeful, complex play that engages the children's full attention

These three levels of play track nicely with Maslow's hierarchy. For example, when children are involved in chaotic and out-of-control play, their safety needs are not being met. They need a sense of safety in order to learn, grow, and change. Unfortunately, I have worked in classrooms where safety was a serious issue. And the children never did engage in high-level play because their safety needs were not satisfied.

In addition to safety needs, children must trust others in order to satisfy their need to belong. Dramatic play in particular often involves much socialization, cooperation, and compromise. When children say, "Let's be friends," or "You be the doggie and I'll be the Mommy," they are feeling a sense of belonging, of community, with the group. Esteem needs are being met in the creativity involved in constructing with manipulatives and blocks that leads to a sense of self-confidence: I can do this! My idea is a good one! Self-actualization can be seen in many kinds of play as children develop a higher sense of cognitive awareness, pulling together information they have learned and using it creatively. For example, children may say, "No, firefighters don't carry guns. They have hoses and ladders so they can save the people in the burning building. Let's go, firefighters!"

It's important for a teacher to observe children at play and determine which of the needs in the hierarchy are most evident. Depending on what the teacher observes, she can then take steps to satisfy that need so the children can move further along. When children engage in creative and imaginative play, they are taking risks with their ideas and interactions with others. Taking risks can be scary. So, effective teachers of young children work hard to establish caring relationships with them and establish a sense of community with the group. Then, children can engage in high-level play confidently and give all of their attention and energy to their play. The teacher has helped them move up the Hierarchy of Needs.

New Information, New Solutions

Another way to consider the levels of children's play is in terms of another theorist's thinking: Jean Piaget's notions of assimilation and accommodation. *Assimilation* involves taking in new information while *accommodation* involves making changes in thinking because of that information. These two processes operate simultaneously as humans have new experiences and take in new information. *Accommodation* drives the motivation to figure things out and solve problems (Labinowicz 1980). In both chaotic and simplistic play, children are more in the assimilation mode than in the accommodation one. They are not using their intellect to modify their thinking or try out new experiences. Thus, there is a limited ability to take new information and apply it in the play experience. Ultimately, this can be frustrating for children and, in their frustration, they may misbehave.

For children to play in ways that are beneficial to them, they must be more in the accommodation process, using their play experiences to accommodate or change their thinking. For example, when children incorporate story lines from books that have been read to them and act them out in their dramatic play scenarios, they often rewrite the plots somewhat and mix characters from various stories. They are accommodating—incorporating new information from the stories and making them their own in their dramatizations. Or when they use vocabulary from their science experiences as they set up ramps in the block area and make predictions about which vehicle will go the farthest, they are accommodating as well.

Accommodation is evident when a child pauses to figure out how to make a wobbly block structure stand or how to get the water wheel to turn as quickly

as possible. And as children use symbols in their play—such as a cylindrical block for a drinking cup or a baby stroller for a lawn mower—they are using abstract thinking to accomplish their play goals. "Play therefore becomes a creative experience in which the child bends reality to his own wishes, incorporating his social experiences, reliving his pleasures, and resolving his conflicts . . ." (Labinowicz 1980, 68). It's important for teachers to observe what children are doing and see if indeed they are engaged in the more complex process of applying new information as they play, in accommodation, rather than assimilation.

Imagination, Roles, and Rules

Lev Vygotsky and his followers also help educators to better understand play. The facilitating of mature, high-level play is exactly what Vygotskians see as "the leading activity of the preschool and kindergarten period" (Bodrova and Leong 2007, 129) and, in particular, make-believe or pretend play. Vygotsky identifies three components of this play. In it, children

1. create an imaginary situation
2. take on and act out roles
3. follow a set of rules determined by the specific roles
   (Bodrova and Leong 2007, 129)

Because the children want to engage in this play, they must regulate their behavior to play the roles correctly, as agreed upon by the group. That's why preschool and kindergarten teachers will hear children disagreeing as they play, saying things like, "No, that's not what the Mommy does. The Mommy has to . . . " or "You can't do that in the grocery store." Children are encouraging each other to play in the right way, the way that fits their conceptions about the roles they are acting out.

Vygotskians say that by the end of kindergarten, truly self-regulated children can think first and act later. They can restrain their own impulses. "This perspective is a different view of play than that denoted by the oft-used phrase 'free play.' As Berk and Winsler state so eloquently, 'Free play is not really 'free' since renouncing impulsive action—that is, not doing just what one wants to do at the moment—is the route to satisfying, pleasurable make-believe.' (1995, 56)" (Bredekamp 2004, 163). So, teachers can facilitate such play, mediate the disagreements, help children verbalize the characteristics of the roles they are playing, and scaffold the play of less-experienced or less-mature players so that they, too, can join in this important process. The development of self-regulation is so important to later academic success—indeed to success in life itself—that teachers have an obligation to help children reach this high level of play.

Examining the quality of children's play at the three levels and incorporating the theoretical frameworks of Maslow, Piaget, and Vygotsky can lead teachers to determine the best strategies to help children reach self-actualization by engaging in successful accommodation and mature, high-level dramatic play.

Chaotic, Out-of-Control Play

I have spent time in early childhood classrooms where safety often became an issue because the children were engaging in chaotic play. How do I know that this is the case? Here are some of the characteristics of chaotic, out-of-control play:

- Children's voices are loud and high-pitched.
- There are high levels of physicality, sometimes bordering on dangerous risk-taking behaviors.
- Sometimes I see extreme hilarity—children are laughing and giggling uncontrollably.
- More disagreements occur, often resulting in physical injury or in hurt feelings.

Although purposeful play also involves noise and physical activity, there is a threshold that is crossed when it deteriorates into chaotic or out-of-control play. Settling children down after such experiences requires the teachers to employ many techniques and strategies and make adjustments that meet the unique personalities within the group of children involved.

The following incident shows how sand play for one group did not move to higher-level play and how it presented safety issues.

Sand Table

Mary Anne, a teacher of three-year-olds, filled the sensory table with sand. She provided small, plastic shovels and containers, thinking the children would explore the properties of sand and estimate how many scoops would be needed to fill various containers. "From the very first day, children's engagement at the sensory table was not positive. Safety became an issue as children began to dig with more and more vigor; the sand was going everywhere, including in children's eyes and on the floor. Children were slipping on the spilled sand. Children's voices grew high-pitched, their digging grew more forceful, and their giggles and howls became more hysterical." Mary Anne and her colleague would try to stay nearby and encourage them to be more gentle in their actions and to describe what the sand looked and felt like, but to no avail. The same behavior happened each day. (Gronlund and James 2008, 104)

When teachers see preschoolers or kindergartners engaged in such chaotic, out-of-control play they must intervene to establish a safe experience for the children. However, in the case above, the intervention efforts of the teachers did not change the nature of the play. Chaotic, out-of-control play continued.

The reaction of some teachers is to discipline the children involved. This may involve separating the group, making them sit in a quiet area removed from all play, or directing them to another activity. And yet, such disciplinary action is rarely needed. Instead of ending the play completely, an adult can provide a sense of control and stability that may very well turn the play away from the chaotic and help the children to complicate it and sustain their interest.

The goal of play facilitation should always be to help children engage in high-level play rather than only intervening to stop chaotic and out-of-control behavior. Even in the case of the sand play above, other interventions could have been tried before closing down the sand table altogether. Separating children, taking away materials, or ending the play should be an intervention of last resort and should only occur after many other attempts have been made to get the children focused in more productive play. It's an important mind-set for teachers to have. Rather than immediately seeing the play as a behavior problem on the part of the children, teachers should ask themselves, "In what ways can I intervene so that the play changes? What can I offer in the way of ideas, materials, or my involvement that will provide safety and control?" Many strategies for doing just that will be shared throughout this book.

Simplistic and Repetitive Play

Simplistic play is different from chaotic, out-of-control play. Safety and noise are rarely issues durig simplistic play, so it may not always grab the teacher's attention. Instead, the play is often repetitive and not very involved. The child may imitate actions that he has seen an adult do, but he does not go beyond that imitation. For toddlers, this type of play is rewarding and appropriate. For preschoolers and kindergartners, however, it is lacking in the qualities of more complex, imaginative play.

> For very young children, who are just beginning to learn that they can perform the same actions they see others performing, imitation can be the first stage of their learning about the power of dramatic play. And older children often effectively use imitation to get started on a new play scene . . . . but the driving force in play is internal. It is dominated by a child's personal interpretation and transformation of outside events. (Carlsson-Paige and Levin 1990, 22)

Simplistic, imitative play is above the safety level on Maslow's Hierarchy of Needs, but it does not necessarily involve the type of social negotiation that comes with extensive role-playing situations. For example, in a role-play situation one child might say, "You were the mommy last time, remember? Now it's my turn. You can be the sister, okay?" Nor does simplistic play require the use of thinking, problem-solving, and other cognitive skills that a sustained, creative play scenario demands. In a more complex play scenario, a child might say, "My block tower is taller than yours. See? It doesn't fall down because I'm the builder. You have to use these big blocks on the bottom, not on the top." Such interactions are not common in simplistic, imitative play. Here's an example of simplistic play in action.

Dramatic Play

Leyonna (4 years 7 months) and Amber (4 years 10 months) are playing in the housekeeping area of the classroom. Teacher Della walks over, sits down at the table, and asks, "What are you girls doing over here?" They immediately begin bringing her cups, saying, "This is orange juice," and plates with plastic pieces of pizza on them. Della pretends to drink and eat, conversing with the girls about what kind of pizza it is and what else they can cook. The girls answer her questions and continue to repeat the same actions again and again. (Gronlund and James 2008, 172)

When teachers observe children engaged in simplistic play, they need to help them move beyond the repetitive actions and get engaged so that their intellect is more challenged. This may mean responding as one might to a toddler, adding vocabulary and providing descriptive commentary as the child repeats actions. Or a teacher may add suggestions or materials, posing questions that lead the child into a higher level as they pretend or use symbolic thinking.

In the situation above, Della could have continued to interact with the girls in this manner, but something was bothering her. She saw that the placing of the plates and glasses on the table was getting wilder and wilder, and she noticed a lack of variety in their ideas for food items to serve. She decided to make some suggestions to see if the play might go beyond its repetitiveness and become more complex and engaging for the girls.

Dramatic Play, continued

Della suggests that they may need to go to the grocery store and get some different things to cook. She wonders aloud if they need to make a grocery list. The girls respond enthusiastically and dictate items for Della to write down on a piece of paper. Della encourages them to look around at the items they have in the housekeeping area so that they can go "shopping." She then provides them with grocery bags, gives them the list, and sends them on their way. The girls stay with this activity for approximately fifteen minutes, checking in with Della even when she is working with other children across the classroom. (Gronlund and James 2008, 172)

In order to recognize simplistic play, a teacher needs to carefully observe as children play. Staying near, watching, and listening as children play helps an observant teacher see the quality of the play interactions. If teachers are busy setting up another activity, preparing for lunch or snack, or leading a small group, they miss opportunities to recognize simplistic play as it occurs and to

facilitate what's happening. In the situation above, Della was able to give the girls ideas and suggestions that added more depth to their play and launched them into a more meaningful and engaging experience. Once the girls were launched, they no longer needed Della's ideas or suggestions. She was able to move on to observe and interact with other children.

Children have moved into more purposeful play when they can sustain their own engagement without the necessity of continuous adult facilitation and support. That does not mean that teachers will not interact with children in higher-level play. Instead, they may find that the interactions take on a different tone. The girls still checked in with Della, even from across the room. Yet they returned to the independent play that she had helped them get started. They did not need her to be a coplayer as she was when being served the pizza and orange juice, nor did they need her to provide additional ideas. The grocery store and shopping list scenario was holding their interest, providing a broad enough range of possibilities for their play over an extended period of time.

In this age of technology and media influences, many young children are experiencing a lot of screen time—watching TV and DVDs and playing computer or video games. But they have not had as many opportunities to engage in dramatic play, block play, or other creative play experiences. They may need to be taught play skills and have chances to practice them. Like a two-year-old who finds great pleasure in knocking down a stack of blocks, a preschool child who has little experience with blocks may also need to try out experiments with gravity. Building and knocking down structures may look like chaotic, out-of-control play, but it may actually be a step in the exploration and practice phase of block play for a child. The child's teacher may need to provide a way for safe "building and knocking down" play for a while before the child can move on to more productive block building.

The same may be true with dramatic play. Children who spend extensive time watching TV may merely imitate scenarios they've seen in favorite cartoons and movies. They may not come up with their own ideas for dramatic play. Unfortunately, their scenarios may involve fighting off "bad guys" and may pose safety issues. Of course, intervention will be needed then. But even more disturbing can be the lack of fresh ideas, new plot twists, and new character possibilities that would complicate this play. Preschool and kindergarten children can quickly grow bored in play that is imitative of their media experiences. "Whenever something is imitated, it must be transformed through play in order to become meaningful and useful information to a child. So, while imitation can play a useful role in development, a problem can result when children get fixated on it and do not transform what they are imitating into play" (Carlsson-Paige and Levin 1990, 22). Teachers will need to intervene to help children move beyond the imitative by suggesting a new script idea: "What if the superheroes found a magic book that told how to make a potion that would keep the bad guys away?" Or they could ask provocative questions, such as "Does the bad guy have a mommy?" "Do you think she loves him?" Or they could suggest new character combinations, such as "What if Barbie met Luke Skywalker and Shrek came to visit with Donkey? What would happen then?"

Children's simplistic and repetitive play may be a result of lack of experiences with rich play or attempts to imitate media experiences that they have had. They are not accommodating new information and ideas, but staying at a shallow and unfulfilling level of play instead. I worry that this kind of play sometimes slips under the radar screen in preschool and kindergarten classrooms. Because it does not always demand a teacher's attention, it may go unnoticed. Then, the children do not get the support they need to move to the more beneficial level of play experiences.

Productive, High-Level Play

Children's productive play is a joy to see and even more fun to be a part of. In high-level play:

- Children are highly engaged for extended periods of time ranging from fifteen minutes to over one hour.
- Children assign roles to each other and play out those roles within the general flow of the play scenario.
- Few behavior problems arise even though disagreements may have to be negotiated and compromises reached. These negotiations are often quick and agreeable.
- The noise level of productive play is at a reasonable volume and can easily be quieted, if necessary, with a brief and friendly reminder.
- Teachers are called upon for specific needs, such as finding an item to complement the play or helping to settle a disagreement so that the play can continue.
- Teachers are called upon to watch and to provide feedback and affirmation. Then the play continues. The teacher's ongoing involvement is rarely needed.
- Materials are used creatively. Real objects are not necessarily needed because a small block can be a cell phone or a stack of connecting cubes can be a fire hose.

This not only happens in dramatic play, but also in block play where one person may present the idea for building: "I know. Let's build a big fort." The child may give others directions for bringing together the right materials into an acceptable design: "No, not that way. It has to go over here so the cars can't get in." Often the other children follow these directions, willingly join in, and demonstrate the self-regulation that Vygotsky talked about.

Sometimes multiple ideas are shared and true cooperative play evolves as children follow through with many different ways of building or pretending to be a family. "Children orchestrate their manipulations of objects, voices, and, indeed, languages themselves as they repeat and extend one another's contributions to the making of a world. Play, then, is a socially complex communicative act" (Genishi and Dyson 2009, 61).

When children are engaged in high-level play, one sees the all-engaging attention that children devote to a complex play experience. They are like athletes "in the zone" or as Mihaly Csikszentmihalyi (1997, 31–32) suggests, they are engaged in a "flow experience." He defines *flow* as: "When a person's entire being is stretched in the full functioning of body and mind, whatever one does becomes worth doing for its own sake. In the harmonious focusing of physical and psychic energy, life finally comes into its own." Even preschoolers and kindergartners can stretch in the full functioning of body and mind when an experience is worth doing, and high-level play can provide just such an experience. Vygotsky saw the child in complex, high-level play as acting beyond his age and standing a head taller than himself. This is why teachers do not see many behavioral problems arise when children are engaged in high-level play. They are fully involved, using so many of their skills and cognitive and social abilities. Because of this deep level of involvement, their safety and belonging needs are well met. They are moving up the Hierarchy of Needs, experiencing high esteem and moving toward self-actualization.

Optimal Flow

The teacher's role in supporting high-level play is critical. Children relish challenge and seek to stretch themselves, but they can be overwhelmed if the challenges are too great, or frustrated if the challenges are not stimulating enough. Good teachers get to know the children in their class well so they can determine the level of challenge that is right for each child's capabilities. In describing more about flow experiences, Csikszentmihalyi talks about the kinds of challenges necessary for optimal flow experiences to occur:

> Flow tends to occur when a person's skills are fully involved in overcoming a challenge that is just about manageable. Optimal experiences usually involve a fine balance between one's ability to act, and the available opportunities for action. If challenges are too high one gets frustrated, then worried, and eventually anxious. If challenges are too low relative to one's skills one gets relaxed, then bored. If both challenges and skills are perceived to be low, one gets to feel apathetic. But when high challenges are matched with high skills, then the deep involvement that sets flow apart from ordinary life is likely to occur. (1997, 30)

Vygotsky defined a zone of proximal development as the area where children can stretch to accomplish something new with adult assistance or scaffolding. This is true as children acquire new skills and understand new concepts, and it is also true in their play experiences. Reaching the higher levels of play may require much adult assistance for some children. In addition, Vygotsky viewed play itself as a zone of proximal development or "a self-help tool that enables children to achieve higher levels of cognitive functioning" (Roskos and Christie 2004, 113). But again, he was talking of high-level, mature play—not play that is chaotic or simplistic.

It's important that teachers think about the conditions that support high-level play and create an environment where children will see many possibilities that stimulate their imaginations and are worthy of their attention. In general, providing a range of interesting and well-organized materials in various play areas, creating an inherent structure for play experiences, and allowing enough time for deep play to develop and be sustained are necessary to promote higher levels of play. Chapter 3 focuses on more in-depth discussion about creating these conditions. And the role of the teacher cannot be forgotten. Although high-level, complex play is often successful without teacher involvement, a teacher can still interact with the children in ways that will sustain and extend the play so that it goes even further.

Remember the sand play situation described earlier in this chapter? Mary Anne and her colleague did come up with some ways to move the children's play beyond a chaotic and out-of-control experience without having to close down the sensory table completely. Here's an example of how to change the conditions for the play in such a way that children become engaged on a much different level and sustain interest over an extended period of time.

Sand Play, continued

Mary Anne and her colleague decided that they needed to give the children more clearly defined reasons to dig in the sand. They went to the library and checked out books on archaeology. They read to the children about how animal remains are found buried in the soil, giving scientists information about life on the earth at different times in the earth's history. They then buried small animal and dinosaur figures in the sand and encouraged the children to carefully dig them

up just like the archaeologists in the book had done. They changed the digging tools from shovels and containers to small brushes and spoons, which encouraged more careful digging as well as more use of fine-motor skills. Once the items were found in the sand, they were sorted and categorized by types of animals, sizes, and when they lived, and charts were made to document what was found. A teacher was nearby each day at the "dig site" so that she could help the children sort and document what they found in the sand. Complexity had been added to the activity, increasing its intellectual engagement and physical challenge, thus settling down the behavior. Mary Anne reported very positive results. (Gronlund and James 2008, 105)

The perspectives of child development theorists can help teachers as they consider ways to enhance children's play experiences. By considering three things about the children—their needs for safety and belonging, the importance of incorporating new ideas into play, and the benefits of role playing in dramatic play—teachers can determine the best ways to lead children away from simplistic or chaotic play to higher, more mature play. The next chapter discusses specific ways that teachers can create an environment in which complex, rich play develops and thrives.

CHAPTER 3

Planning for Play

> Teachers provide experiences, materials, and interactions to enable
> children to engage in play that allows them to stretch their boundaries to
> the fullest in their imagination, language, interaction, and self-regulation
> as well as to practice their newly acquired skills. (NAEYC Position
> Statement on DAP, Guideline #2.E.4, Copple and Bredekamp 2009, 18)

Maria has decided that there is no such thing as "free play" in her preschool
classroom. She spends too much time planning for the children's play experiences to consider it a truly "free" time. She has carefully organized the play
areas and chosen the materials for each area, sometimes adding new things to
interest the children and to take their play in a different direction. On her lesson
plans she writes goals for play, so the goal for the block area this week might
be "names and recognizes geometric shapes." Maria watches carefully so she
can see progress in action. She interacts with the children by asking questions
that lead them to use their verbal and problem-solving skills, or apply their
understanding of geometry and other concepts. She calls playtime "Investigation
Time" and allows forty-five minutes to an hour of each morning and afternoon
for it in her daily schedule. And she communicates to families how she plans for
play experiences that are challenging so that they understand as well: playtime
is not a time for free play (as in chaotic, out-of-control play), but rather a time
for productive, engaged, high-level play to occur.

To help preschool and kindergarten children move toward higher levels
of play, teachers like Maria create conditions that will provide safety, encourage imaginative thinking, and support sustained interest. That means that

teachers must plan for play! Even though the goal is for children to have flow experiences where they are deeply engaged in directing their own actions in productive ways, teachers must take the following important steps that will lead children to go with the flow in their play:

- Teachers set up the environment.
- Teachers provide an inherent structure for play.
- Teachers allow enough time in the daily schedule for deep play to develop.

This chapter focuses on the ways teachers can create a well-ordered environment and provide engaging materials so that young children can take risks. By thinking about and planning for play, teachers help children create play scenarios where they can lose themselves in the roles they act out or in the creations they are designing. In addition, teachers strategically interact with children to enhance and sustain their play. This is discussed in more depth in later chapters.

Create a Well-Ordered Environment

How teachers arrange the room and present materials are important aspects of planning for play. By organizing the room into distinct spaces, they are helping children know exactly what materials are available in each area and in what ways they can use those materials. Most preschool and kindergarten classrooms include the following areas: blocks, dramatic play, manipulatives, art, sensory table, class library, and writing table. Some also have a distinct science or math area, an area for musical instruments, a listening area, and perhaps a "quiet zone" or area to rest. The separateness and organization of each area provides a sense of security and clarity of purpose to children. Blocks are for building; dramatic play is for pretending; manipulatives are for creating. In contrast, teachers in classrooms with poorly defined areas often see more negative behavior on the part of the children. The environment in these classrooms is not providing clear signals and boundaries for the use of materials. A well-organized classroom communicates a sense of order and structure, and it offers a wide range of possibilities to stimulate imaginative use of materials.

These photographs show how some teachers have organized the areas of their classrooms into distinct places for play and exploration.

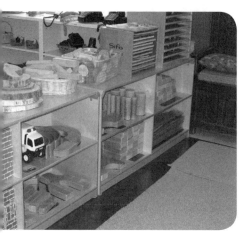

In well-organized classrooms, shelves and tables are laid out in such a way as to create a space large enough to accommodate three or four children. A rug or masking tape on the floor can help define the area. Placing a bin of materials on a tablecloth or piece of fabric on the floor can define another area for play. Traffic patterns are a primary consideration so that children's constructions in the block area are not at risk of being toppled by children moving from one area to another. Shelves are placed to close off long, open areas of the classroom that might otherwise encourage running. Quieter areas are grouped together (such as the class library, listening center, writing center, and art area) so that the noisier activities of blocks and dramatic play do not distract or interfere with the children who are reading, writing, or creating. The following classroom map gives one example of room arrangement strategies in action.

As illustrated in this classroom arrangement, some areas are defined by shelving, some by rugs, and some by masking tape.

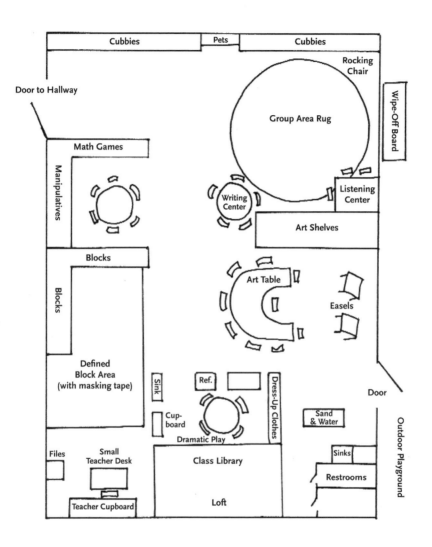

Of course, preschool and kindergarten teachers face practical realities when deciding how to set up their classroom space. The locations of doors and windows, electrical outlets, and radiators must be addressed. All teachers do their best with the facilities available to them. It's best to place the computer near the electrical outlets, and the art area near water for easy cleanup. It's also important to be ready to rearrange the room if problems arise in any area. Room arrangement is a work in progress in most classrooms!

There are many good resources available that provide excellent suggestions for arranging the classroom. Consider investigating these for more ideas:

- *The Creative Curriculum for Preschool,* 4th ed., by Diane Trister Dodge, Laura Colker, and Cate Heroman
- *Creating Inclusive Classrooms* by Ellen R. Daniels and Kay Stafford
- *Reflecting Children's Lives: A Handbook for Planning Child-Centered Curriculum* by Deb Curtis and Margie Carter
- *The Inclusive Early Childhood Classroom: Easy Ways to Adapt Learning Centers for All Children* by Patti Gould and Joyce Sullivan
- *Big as Life: The Everyday Inclusive Curriculum* by Stacey York
- *Designs for Living and Learning: Transforming Early Childhood Environments* by Deb Curtis and Margie Carter
- *Classroom Routines that Really Work for PreK and Kindergarten* by Kathleen Hayes and Reneé Creange

Provide Materials that Will Engage the Children

Making a range of interesting materials available in each of the play areas of the classroom is the next step to facilitate more engaging play. So that problems with sharing don't develop, it is critical that there are enough materials for a number of children to use. And it helps to organize the materials in such a way that children can easily access them. Shelves should be low so the children can reach them, and they should be filled with bins and baskets of manipulatives, art, and writing materials. Many teachers organize their wooden blocks and manipulatives on shelves with picture labels so children know what goes where. The dramatic play area includes a place for hanging dress-up clothes and cupboards for storing dishes and play foods. Some teachers hang tools near a sensory table (in a shoe hanger with plastic sleeves) so children can easily see them and choose a scooper, a teaspoon, a funnel, or a small cup when playing with water or sand.

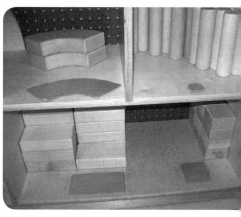

To encourage more imaginative use of materials, teachers will find it's better to offer more open-ended materials than close-ended materials. Children can use open-ended materials in multiple ways and be successful in using them. Close-ended materials offer only one right way to use them. While there's nothing wrong with having puzzles and matching games available, these materials are all close-ended. Children will experience less frustration and develop more creativity and problem-solving skills with open-ended materials. Some common open-ended materials for preschool and kindergarten classrooms are offered below:

- blocks
- dress-up clothes
- kitchen items
- manipulatives such as Legos; small, colored blocks; various kinds of connectors
- clay or playdough and many different kinds of papers (construction, tissue, lined and unlined writing paper, wallpaper)
- writing and drawing tools (markers, pens, pencils, crayons, chalks, paints)

Many teachers find that bringing in boxes with odds and ends (such as paper towel rolls or fabric scraps) and providing tape, staplers, and other items for fastening things together entices children to make and build items to accompany their play and enhance their pretending.

The materials in a classroom should also reflect the cultural lives of the children there as well as provide a window on the world outside of their experience. Baby dolls and people figures should be multiracial—reflecting the diversity of the world—whether the children in the group are diverse racially or not. Home living items should include things the children experience in their homes. The following are some examples:

- In some American Indian preschools the home area is called a "hogan" and is set up as such. Weaving looms are included and children often imitate their family members weaving blankets as they do in their own homes.

- In communities where hunting is common, children may use blocks as guns to hunt deer and then pretend to prepare the venison for eating. Rather than forbidding such play, teachers work with the children, talking about gun safety and hunting experiences that they have had.

- In a classroom in central Indiana, a few of the children made complex Lego constructions to represent combines that plow the fields and harvest the crops at their family farms. Four-year-olds could describe in detail the different parts of the combine in their constructions.

- A friend and colleague, Marlyn James, tells stories of children in rural Montana playing at cutting wood with pretend chainsaws and asking teachers to fill the gas tanks on their tricycles. In fact, they not only ask for one tank to be filled, but also the extra tank since distances in Montana are extensive and many folks have two tanks in their cars and trucks.

Being aware of the children's experiences in their communities and introducing materials that reflect others' experiences are important considerations for teachers as they stock their shelves and dramatic play areas.

Change Materials

Some teachers think it is necessary to rearrange the classroom or provide new materials and activities every day or every week. This is not the case! It's too much change for the children and too much work for the teacher. Instead, the children's engagement should be the cue for determining when to change. This means that teachers must continually evaluate the children's involvement in each of the areas. If they observe that play is rich and engaging, that interest is sustained, and that few behavioral problems arise, they may determine that no changes are needed because the materials and space are working well.

"If the original materials provided in an area include a range of possibilities, the children should be able to return again and again and become engaged in productive and creative use of those materials" (Gronlund 2003, 28). However, if teachers notice that children are not choosing an area or are not using it well, they may find that by changing the materials, they offer new possibilities that will ignite children's interest once again. Here are some of the behaviors that can signal that a change in an area may be needed:

- The children are ignoring a particular area.
- The children are bored with what's available (they may say they are bored; they may appear bored in their interactions; or they may change the area themselves, bringing new materials or doing different things with those materials).
- The children's behavior is not productive or positive in an area.

- The materials could be changed to support an interest of the children, a developmental need, or a topic of study or project that has emerged in the classroom.
  (Gronlund 2003, 27–28)

Rotating materials and adding additional materials periodically provokes more interest in an area and helps children develop a variety of combinations in their play. Placing measuring tapes and yardsticks in a block area, cookbooks and grocery circulars in the play kitchen, and photographs of various types of vehicles in the manipulatives area may stimulate children's thinking. Many teachers put together "prop boxes" to transform the dramatic play area from a family home to a hospital, restaurant, or veterinarian's office. The decision to bring out a particular set of props may be based on interests shown by the children, upcoming field trips or special visitors, or just the perception that a change is needed. (For a good list of suggested props to include for a variety of prop box themes, see *Play: The Pathway from Theory to Practice* by Sandra Heidemann and Deborah Hewitt, pages 35–37 and 139).

How long should a set of props be available for play? Again, it depends on the engagement of the children. If they're still playing with them in a productive way, there's no need to change. If they aren't, maybe a change in props would help. I knew a teacher who provided props for veterinarian play because her children were acting out taking care of the few stuffed animals she had available. She added more animals, stethoscopes, bandages, animal cages, and leashes. For several weeks the children engaged in rich, sustained play tending to the medical needs of the stuffed animals. But one day, much to this teacher's surprise, they took it upon themselves to pack up the box of props and turn the dramatic play area back into a family home. Cooking and tending to babies became the focus of their pretend play once again!

Rotating materials on the shelves can keep the available choices interesting and not overwhelming for the children. Bringing out a marble run or set of gears periodically, instead of daily, will keep these activities fresh and new. Changing the connecting manipulatives for creating constructions and vehicles (from Legos to Bristle Blocks to magnetic blocks) will stimulate different ways for children to use fine-motor skills and express imaginative ideas. Teachers often change the sensory material in their sensory table to keep children's interest and engagement. Water and sand are staples that may very well engage the children for weeks. Changing to seeds, pebbles, or potting soil provides different sensory experiences.

Sometimes the materials should be changed because they are just not engaging enough to lend themselves to high-level play. Consider the following story from a preschool classroom:

Water Table

Four children are gathered around the water table. In the water are rocks and toothbrushes. The children scrub the rocks vigorously with the brushes and talk among themselves about getting them clean. Soon, the children's attention begins to wander and each one looks around the room even as they continue to scrub the rocks. Shortly thereafter, they lose interest altogether, remove their plastic smocks, and choose another area in which to play.

The materials provided only one possibility to the children: scrubbing and getting the rocks clean. There were no other ways to use them, so the children's initial interest waned quickly. They did not use the materials inappropriately as in chaotic, out-of-control play. Instead, they stayed at a simplistic play level and did not become fully engaged. Often, short attention to an activity results because there is just not enough complexity to it. In order to engage children's sustained interest, teachers need to choose materials that have many possibilities. Washing and scrubbing rocks with brushes did not have such possibilities. Here are some ways that the activity could have been more complex.

- A variety of brushes, sponges, and cloths could be provided and, in addition to rocks, other natural items could be placed in the water (such as pine cones, sticks, shells, and seed pods). Then, comparisons could be made between which tool works best on which object and which items float and sink.
- The activity could be set up for children to wash and scrub the rocks, then place them on a drying rack and look at the differences in their appearance as they dried. They could be encouraged to try this more than once to note the differences. Their descriptions of the rocks' appearance when wet and dry could be recorded on a class chart or with photo documentation.
- The children could paint the rocks with tempera or watercolor paints, then wash and scrub them noting the changes in their appearance as well as the appearance of the water. They could be

encouraged to notice how hard they must scrub and how long it takes for the paint to come off.

There are times when adding new materials along with a new idea or two on how to use the materials is the only strategy a teacher needs to lead children to more sustained involvement. There are other times when the teacher must get involved in the play to lead the children to more in-depth engagement. It is important to pay attention to the children's cues when they remain in simplistic play and to be ready to add more complexity to the activity.

Write Plans for Play

Certainly, thinking about room arrangement and materials is an important part of planning for play. In addition, teachers should write down plans for the play environment and props. Often, teachers only write on their plans what they will do with the children in small- and large-group experiences, what the art activities will be, which books will be read, and which songs will be sung. All of these aspects of the program are important. But writing down plans for the play areas, such as blocks, dramatic play, manipulatives, and sensory table, is as important.

The lesson plan should include the goals that teachers have in mind for each of the play areas and the materials they will need to provide to meet those goals. In some lesson planning frameworks (*Creative Curriculum for Preschool, Focused Early Learning*), spaces are provided for each of the play areas so teachers can record goals and materials. Here is an example of a plan for play from *Focused Early Learning* (Gronlund 2003, 30).

Child-led Exploration in the Rich Classroom Environment

Blocks
Respect other's work & ideas as children construct & build

Dramatic Play
Use expressive language to imitate household tasks & family life

Manipulatives
Use planning skills with small items

Art
Identify colors & shapes while experimenting with paints, markers, scissors & paste

Ongoing Projects

Exploring the classroom

Sensory Table
Use measurement words (more, less, bigger, smaller) with water & measurement tools

Library
Show interest in books & awareness of print

Writing Center
Use writing tools to make marks in imitation of writing & letter-like marks

---

A written record such as this helps teachers in more ways than one. It requires teachers to reflect and to think back on the ways children have been using the areas. Questions such as "What's working well?" and "What's not working?" lead teachers to determine what needs to be changed and what can stay as is. If the children are using an area well and if their play there is at a high, sustained level, then no changes need to be made. However, if either chaotic or simplistic play is evident, changes are necessary. Therefore, the "What's not working?" question needs to be addressed in the plan for the following week.

Writing down plans that incorporate goals can guide teachers in their interactions with the children while they play at that area. If the goal at the manipulatives area is to use planning skills with small items, teachers can encourage children to identify a plan as they construct there. A teacher might ask, "What do you think you might make with the Legos today?" If a child is having a hard time with this planning process and says, "I want to make a school bus but I don't know how," the two could discuss where the child might find information (such as in books and Internet resources) that would be helpful and the complexity of the manipulative play would be increased. Chapter 8 explores in-depth the process of incorporating goals and early learning standards more fully into children's play.

And finally, a written lesson plan for play areas gives teachers an ongoing record that they can refer to again and again. They may find that they have not added any new materials in the block area for several weeks, or that the dramatic play about hospitals has lasted more than a month. The written plan becomes a way to see where sustained interest and engagement happen or where problems arise. The plan informs the reflection process and deepens the conversations that teaching teams can have as they figure out next steps to support and enhance children's play.

By organizing the environment, providing engaging materials, and changing them when appropriate, teachers are setting up conditions to support children's high-level play. These are carefully thought-out actions that can be written on lesson plans. Teachers plan for play! In the next chapter, another way to plan for play is explored: helping children make positive choices for play experiences.

CHAPTER 4

Ways to Help Children Make Choices

> Teachers present children with opportunities to make meaningful choices, especially in child-choice activity periods. They assist and guide children who are not yet able to enjoy and make good use of such periods. (Copple and Bredekamp 2009, 18)

Amy has decided to structure the way children choose play areas with her class of four-year-olds. She has been noticing that they often choose the same areas again and again. Favorites are evident! But the play she sees in these favorite areas is not always positive and productive. For example, Charlie and Jonathan often choose blocks but then get into conflict as they build and construct. Marna and Tenisha love playdough but don't create interesting pieces. Instead, they make the same pancakes again and again.

Amy introduces a play plan to the children and asks them to color in the area that they are going to play in one day a week. This involves thought, discussion, and consideration as she has decided to encourage the children to choose something other than their favorite area for that one day. At first, they protest. But they seem to like the idea of making plans with friends, recruiting others to join them, and representing their choice on the plan. Amy sees more productive play happen not only on the one day a week that she uses this new procedure, but also on the other days where open choices are allowed and favorite areas are available.

Sometimes teachers think of play as an unstructured time of the day. However, as the last chapter discussed, a carefully arranged environment and presentation of materials is a form of structure, giving clear messages to the children about how spaces are used and materials are organized. This chapter looks at several other things teachers can do to provide structure that helps children successfully reach higher levels of play:

- help children make constructive decisions when choosing play areas
- make clear the procedures for use of the materials in each learning area
- have agreed-upon signals to get children's attention
- allow enough time for deep play to develop

Help Children Make Meaningful Choices

Choice is an important aspect in a program for young children. Young children relish being self-directive. They are in a developmental stage where they are gaining independence from adults and trying things out for themselves, moving toward greater and greater competence. But children do *not* want to do so without the support of adults. They look to their teachers and parents to provide reasonable choices for them so they will be safe and successful in their explorations.

It is important for preschool and kindergarten teachers to think in terms of structuring children's choices so they move beyond chaotic or simplistic play into deeper and broader investigations of their world. Therefore, as discussed in the previous chapters, there is no such thing as free play, nor are there free choices. Instead, teachers have carefully considered what choices are available—choices of areas in which to play, choices of materials available in each area, and choices of ways to use those materials. Children do not have the choice to go to the block area and throw wooden blocks up in the air. Teachers will intervene and guide them to much safer and more productive ways to use the blocks by building and stacking. Children do not have the choice to destroy the dramatic play area, throwing all of the cooking items and dress-up clothes on the floor. Teachers will intervene and help them use the materials to pretend they are cooking, cleaning, or taking care of babies and home.

Establish Procedures for Making Choices

How do teachers make it clear to the children that they want them to choose for themselves, but within a structure of some sort? Choosing activities should be based on a routine process where teachers present a cafeteria-style selection of the possibilities available in the classroom that day. Before playtime, teachers gather the children together in either large or small groups. Then, before dismissing them to play, they verbally walk them through the areas of the classroom that are available. They give reminders of the materials in each area and offer suggestions for ways to use them, thus providing guidance for the choice process and helping those children who may not make positive choices. The same choices may not be available every day, because teachers know that a variety of possibilities keeps children's interest and encourages them to consider areas other than their favorites. As choices are introduced, the teachers highlight the many things that children can do in the classroom much like a salesperson might do to sell a consumer on the qualities of a new car or a vacation package. An enthusiastic tone of voice helps as the "pitch" is made. And having a predictable routine, such as going around the classroom in a visual circle pointing to each area, helps children think through their choices and verbalize a plan.

This is planning for play! The teacher is asking the children to plan—and is making clear that they can't do just anything; the areas and the materials have been carefully planned. Calling the time period for such play something other than "free play" helps to communicate to the children and the parents that a structured set of choices has been provided. Teachers have a variety of names for playtime, including Investigation Time, Exploration Time, Choice Time, and Activity Time. Notice how each of these names communicates a more inherent structure than total freedom and chaotic, out-of-control play.

For many young children, the cafeteria-style selection for play works fine. For others, it does not provide enough structure for them to make productive choices. There are additional ways that teachers can structure the choice process. In deciding which option might work best, a teacher must consider the needs of the particular group of children. Options for structuring the choice process include

- letting the children verbally decide where they want to play and not placing any limits on the grouping of children (open choices)

- limiting the number of children per area
- using a Choosing Board of some kind so that children have a way of physically representing their plan
- making some choices for children and allowing them to make others (have to's and can do's)

A teacher may use one of these options at a time, or may find that combining them works best. Flexibility is important when considering ways to offer choices to the children.

Help Children Make Open Choices

When children have the opportunity to decide for themselves where they want to play (open choices), they are empowered and self-directed. For four- and five-year-olds, this is a wonderful experience and can lead to opportunities for much social negotiation, sharing, and cooperation. And, "Children often choose learning areas for good reasons. The area may represent a strength or interest for that child, may have opportunities to practice skills the child is trying to master, may be a playmate's favorite, or may have something the child has not tried before" (Gronlund 2003, 90).

Here's an example of the Open Choice system at its best:

Playdough in a Kindergarten Classroom

One spring day at large-group time, kindergarten teacher Julia described to her students the choices available at Investigation Time that day. One option was to work with playdough and a variety of tools (rollers, wooden pounders, cookie cutters in a variety of shapes, and scissors) at a rectangular table with six chairs around it. In Julia's classroom, the children had the opportunity to choose any area that was available. There were no limits placed on the number of children in an area. As the children stated their plans for their first investigation, Julia noticed that the playdough was attracting a lot of interest. She wondered to herself how the children might work out sharing the materials and space available. As the last child in the group made his choice, Julia glanced over to the playdough table and saw that nine children had gathered around, six sitting and three standing. One of the girls who was standing brought over a chair from another table. As she approached with it, the other children shifted their chairs so there would be room for her. No comments were made—they just moved quietly. The other two children standing also got chairs from elsewhere in the classroom, and the group accommodated them as well.

Two large balls of playdough were in plastic tubs with lids, one at each end of the table. The children at each end opened the tubs and began passing out the playdough so that each of the nine children would have some. Negotiation was needed as amounts were compared. The discussion remained calm, and children broke off pieces of their own chunks in order to give some to children with less. In the end, the group settled down and got to work, rolling, pounding, and cutting their playdough and talking with each other about what they were making.

Julia marveled at the fact that she never had to get involved and walked over to compliment the children on the sharing and cooperation she had observed.

There are many benefits to providing open choices for children. This group had to problem solve (get more chairs, move to fit others, provide similar amounts of playdough) and work together in order to play at the playdough table. And they were successful in doing so! A sense of competence and satisfaction could be seen on their faces, especially as Julia complimented them. But Julia would be the first one to acknowledge that such success does not happen all the time. Since this was spring and these were five-year-olds now turning six, she knew their experiences with cooperation were extensive. She also remembered the many times when problems arose with open choice situations that needed her support and involvement. So, she was observant and ready to step in and intervene if necessary as she had done many times in the past, and she was delighted when the children worked out the situation for themselves.

Open choices may not be the right way to go for all groups of children. Three-year-olds and younger four-year-olds may be overwhelmed by open choices and not have the social skills to handle the negotiating and sharing seen in the kindergarten scene above. Individuals within any age group of children may not be able to handle waiting until the playdough is divided, or sharing personal space at the table. A teacher must know the children in her group to determine whether to offer open choices. However, working toward open choices so that children have the opportunities to try out such high-level social skills is a good goal to have, especially as four-year-olds are turning five and in kindergarten classrooms.

Place Limits on Areas

Some teachers find that it helps to look at the areas of the classroom and think in terms of how much space is available. Then, they determine how many children could work comfortably in that space together. They communicate these limits in different ways. Some teachers post the numeral—as a recommendation—that tells how many children can play in that area at one time. For example, the block area may have a large 4 on the wall, while the listening area may have a 2. Some may also put child figure cutouts next to the numerals so the children can count to determine the quantity of children suggested for that area. Other teachers place a certain number of chairs in the area to communicate the limit. For some, six chairs at the playdough table would mean that the limit was six children there.

Such limits must be communicated clearly to the children as they make their choices. In the announcement of learning areas, materials, and activities for the day, the teacher reminds children how many may choose blocks or puzzles first. She then needs to keep track as children make their choices. It takes some attention on the part of the teacher to make this choosing system work effectively. Here's one way a teacher organized the choosing process so that the children were clear on the number that could choose any given area:

Choosing Time

Each day when she arrived at the preschool, Irene would look at her lesson plan to remind herself of the learning areas and activities that she and her colleagues had planned for Exploration Time that day. In a small plastic basket, she gathered items from those areas that would illustrate the choices available to the children. She chose the same number of items as the number of children identified to fit the space of each area. Then, as she introduced the choices to the children, she pulled out the items to show them the number of children who could choose that area at a time. She showed the children four blocks, five plates from the dramatic play area, three items for weighing at the balance scale, four paintbrushes for painting at the easel, and four napkins for the open snack table. As children announced their choices to start their Exploration Time, they took one of the items from Irene to their designated area. Now Irene could keep track when an area was full and tell children that they would need to make a different choice. She also could watch to see when an opening occurred in their first choice area later in the Exploration Time.

A word of caution is needed here for teachers who consider limiting the number of children in areas. There have been instances when having an additional child in an area did not cause a problem at all for the children there. So why limit them? If children's engagement in an area is positive and productive, a teacher should not worry if there are one or two more children than the identified limit. Instead, she should rejoice that they are doing so well in their play and focus on ways to support them. The limits on some areas are used as a preventive measure so problems don't arise. If there are only two headphones in the listening area, it will be difficult for more than two children to participate and hear well. However, in blocks and dramatic play, the space may very well accommodate more than the identified number of children. And some play scenarios need more players to enhance and complicate the story line. Being flexible and using common sense should guide teachers when they consider limiting children's choices of areas.

One option for areas where materials are limited (such as the listening center) is to suggest that children write their names on a waiting list for that area. This provides reassurance to the child who is waiting and is a meaningful writing experience too. The teacher can have the children's name cards available so they can copy or represent their name as best they can. Then, as the children at the area finish their work there, they are responsible for looking at the next name on the waiting list and going to get that child so he or she can decide whether to join the area. If the child does come to that area, he or she crosses out his or her name on the waiting list. This is another way to provide inherent structure for children's choices and participation in experiences throughout the classroom.

Use Choosing Boards

Another way to structure the choosing process is to have a Choosing Board. Many teachers have a bulletin board or pocket chart with a list of the learning areas of the classroom. The names of the areas are accompanied by a photo or drawing for easy recognition by the children. As teachers go through an explanation of the choices available for that day, they can reference the list, pointing to the names of the areas as they talk about the materials available and the suggested activities. When children choose an area, they come to the Choosing Board and either place something to represent their choice next to the name of the area or take a ticket or representational object to the area itself. Teachers might have each child place something on the Choosing Board next to the name of the area, such as

- a photograph of the child
- a name card
- a clothespin or other form of marker

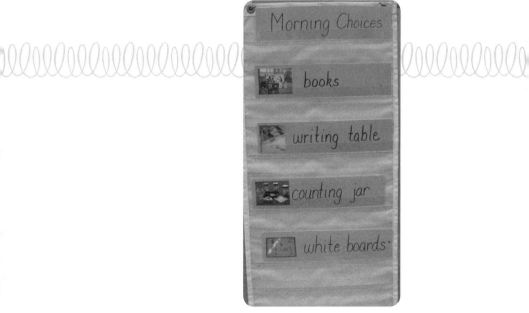

Teachers who have children take away something from the Choosing Board to the area might have them take one of the following items and place it in a designated set of pockets, a bin, or a basket in the area:

- a photo of the area
- a ticket that says the name of the area
- a name card

Or a teacher may have the children who are playing in an area wear one of the following:

- a clothespin or some other form of marker color-coordinated to each area
- a necklace made of a piece of yarn and a lid from a plastic margarine container with the name of the area on it

Choosing Boards add representation to the choosing process and communicate that making choices is an important task. They can work successfully when children make open choices as well as when teachers choose to limit the

number of spots available. Limits on the number of children in an area can be suggested by the number of spaces available on the board. Some teachers only use the Choosing Board for the first choice of the play period. Others have children continue to return to the board to make their second and third choices. For example, a teacher may have the children wear the necklaces suggested above. Some are wearing the block area necklace and, as they finish up their work with the blocks, they return their necklaces to the Choosing Board and choose a necklace from another area. This takes some coordination and direction by teachers until children get the hang of this ongoing choosing process. Providing the Choosing Board for even one choice of the day is a form of giving structure to the choosing process and play experience. The process also communicates the importance of children's choices.

Make Some Choices for Children

High-level play does not develop in all play situations, and teachers have important roles in helping children move to deep and sustained play experiences. At times it may be wise for teachers to provide a balance of choices so that children make some choices about their play activities and teachers make others for them. These teacher-made choices are often teacher-guided activities, ones where adult involvement is needed (such as in cooking or conducting a science experiment) as well as ones where the adult might be a play facilitator, trying to get some new things going or providing some behavioral guidance to a particular group of children. Young children will rebel if all choices are made for them. Their desire for independence and drive to feel competent and capable will butt up against total adult direction. Finding just the right balance between children following their own interests and teacher-guided experiences is a challenge.

In the NAEYC Position Statement on Developmentally Appropriate Practice, both adult-guided and child-guided experiences are valued: "Children benefit *both* from engaging in self-initiated, spontaneous play *and* from teacher-planned and structured activities, projects, and experiences" (Copple and Bredekamp 2009, 49). By having occasional times in the classroom for the choice process to be structured between child-initiated activities and teacher-guided ones, a teacher may find that optimal, developmentally appropriate balance.

Sometimes a teacher must make choices for a child because the choices he or she is making are not positive ones. Consider these examples:

- A child who consistently throws sand at the faces of other children outdoors may need to have the choice of sand play taken away for a time.
- A child who dominates dramatic play in such a way that other children get frustrated because they cannot contribute to the "script" or participate in ways that interest them may need adult help in listening to the ideas of others.

In both of these examples, a teacher takes away the child's choices and offers other choices because it is in the child's best interest at the time. It is not done as punishment, but as a temporary suspension of a particular choice because it was causing problems for that child and for others. The teacher reassures the child that there will be another chance to show that the child can remember the procedures of sand play or can demonstrate ways to work together in figuring out dramatic play scenarios. It's important that the teacher watch closely to provide another opportunity for the child to successfully engage in the activity where problems had arisen. That way, the teacher is helping to ensure that the child will make more positive choices in the future.

Some teachers call teacher-determined choices "Have to's" and child-determined ones "Can do's." A "Have to" activity does not necessarily need to be a task-oriented one or take place in a teacher-led group. Teachers may decide that they want all the children to experience the shaving cream in the sensory table and may make that a "Have to" (either for that day or ongoing throughout the week). Or they may want to get some different types of constructions going in the manipulatives area and may show the children color photographs of various types of rescue vehicles. The "Have to" activity is to construct a rescue vehicle of their own out of connecting materials. Sometimes the "Have to" activities are done just to encourage children to interact with different children. Teacher-determined groupings can extend children's social relationships and encourage them to move out of their comfort zones. Here's another example of helping children break out of their routines to choose activities they don't usually do:

The Golden Ticket

At St. Saviour's Church Nursery School in Old Greenwich, Connecticut, the teachers implemented a system for structuring choices that changed the children's favorite play areas as well as helped them build new friendships. In discussions at staff meetings and in informal teaching team conversations, a group of preschool teachers reflected on the success of children's engagement during their hour-long Exploration Time. They realized that many of the children gravitated toward favorite areas and often did not try others. Some children appeared to be stuck in a rut, making the same choices again and again, while others wandered from one center to the next, not engaging fully in the activities and materials provided. The teachers decided to launch something they called the Golden Ticket.

At circle time on select days, the teachers enthusiastically announced to the children that it was a special day and showed them simply decorated and laminated "tickets" with the names and pictures of different learning areas on them. In dramatic and expressive voices, the teachers said things like, "Everyone is going to receive a Golden Ticket today to start our Exploration Time. The ticket might be to your favorite place to play and explore—or it might be to an area that you don't choose very often. This way, you'll be able to find out all of the interesting things that you can do in every area in the classroom. You won't know exactly who else will be in your area until all of the Golden Tickets are passed out.

It will be a big surprise!" The teachers asked the children to remain in their Golden Ticket center for the first twenty minutes of Exploration Time (a set of chimes rang at the end of that period) and informed the children that when they heard the chimes, they could move on to another area or choose to stay where they were.

Careful consideration was given to the children's assignments. The teachers chose centers for various children in order to mix up the places in which they played (between familiar and unfamiliar) as well as to change the peers with whom they interacted. Three or four children were assigned to a center: one would be a frequent visitor to that particular area while the others would have rarely been observed there. The teachers felt that this grouping allowed the child who was familiar with the materials to take more of a leadership role in the group.

On the first day, the children responded with excitement to the announcement of the Golden Tickets. Their excitement about the process was equally divided between the area specified on their ticket and which other children they might find there—good friends or new ones? Teachers were pleased with the response and began to use the Golden Ticket strategy at least once weekly. Over time, the results were remarkable. Frequently, the children who were unlikely to be coaxed into a particular center in the past became quite engaged with the new materials. Often when the Golden Ticket period was over they stayed in that center continuing their exploration and deepening their involvement. The new groupings of children in the centers opened new partnerships within the class. Children who had not spent much time with other children made new connections with each other over unfamiliar materials. Frequently, these new social connections solidified as the children sought each other out on the playground or in other classroom activities. And children who were reticent to share their knowledge in teacher-led group times now freely shared their expertise with peers while comfortably engaged with familiar materials. This allowed their friends to see them in a new light.

Finally, the success of this strategy stimulated the creativity and imagination of the teachers, who became both intentional and playful in designing a host of versatile strategies that could support the children's acquisition of social and other skills. Additional strategies such as Twin for a Day, Mystery Partners, and Special Friend Day enlivened the classrooms and continued to help children interact with new friends in new activities. But the Golden Ticket was still the favorite for both teachers and children.

Procedures for Learning Areas

In most preschool and kindergarten classrooms, teachers and children determine reasonable rules and procedures to help things run smoothly and to provide an inherent structure for safety as children play. Keeping rules as simple and broad as possible, as well as phrasing them in positive language, make them more memorable for the children and easier to enforce for the teachers. "Even at the preschool level, the teacher can formulate guidelines such as these with the class and can use them as reminders and teaching points with children, both individually and in groups" (Gartrell 2004, 71). Three simple rules such as the following can encompass most behaviors and expectations:

1. We keep ourselves safe.
2. We take good care of our classroom inside and out.
3. We help each other.

These rules are broad enough to cover most instances and can serve as friendly reminders for children to learn to regulate their own behavior. It is not necessary to have additional rules for the learning areas of the classroom. However, it often helps if teachers make clear the procedures for use and care of the materials in each learning area. And these procedures may contribute to the development of higher-level play.

When introducing new children to a classroom, a teacher may want to take them on a "field trip" to see all of the places to explore. In visiting each area, the teacher can discuss special considerations that must be taken into account when playing there. For example, the sensory table will have different procedures than the block area. Sand or water on the floor around the sensory table may make it slippery and dangerous for children. Then they wouldn't be able to keep themselves safe (Rule 1 above). So in order to meet that rule, children will need to be careful about spilling sand or water on the floor and clean it up when it does spill. That way, they will also be taking good care of the classroom and helping each other (Rules 2 and 3).

The block area may have picture labels and special baskets for certain sizes and shapes of blocks. In order to meet Rules 2 and 3, cleanup in the block area will need to focus on placing blocks back where they belong, so that cylindrical blocks are on the correct shelf and small pattern blocks are in their labeled basket. Friendly reminders about the procedures at the different learning areas can be part of the introduction of choices for the day. As a teacher sends off the first four children who chose to paint in the art area, she might say, "Don't forget to wear your paint smocks and to write your name on your painting so we know it's yours before you put it in the drying rack." The children have some reasonable responsibilities while creating colorful masterpieces at the easels.

If serious problems develop in a play area, it may be that the procedures for that area need to be revisited. The teacher can call together the group of children involved and review with them the special considerations for that area. If block constructions are continually being knocked over in the block area, the discussion might focus on ways to follow Rule 3. The teacher might ask, "How can we help each other in the block area? What do we need to think about when we are moving back to the shelf to get more blocks for our own constructions?" The children involved may think of ways to build their constructions farther away from the shelves so that everyone can get to the materials they need. Then, more sustained play can develop because the structures are not disturbed.

Signals to Get Children's Attention

Sometimes it may be necessary to address problems arising in play experiences at a class meeting where all of the children can weigh in and offer solutions. And with young children, waiting until later in the day may not have the same effect as dealing with the issue right at the time that it arises. Therefore, it's necessary for teachers to have agreed-upon signals to get children's attention while they are engaged in play activities. Teachers use many different types of signals for this purpose. Some examples are

- clapping a rhythmic pattern over and over until all the children are doing so as well

- ringing a triangle, small set of chimes, or bells until all of the children are quiet and looking at the teacher
- saying a chant such as "Boys and girls, one, two, three, all eyes are on me" (which may need to be said more than once)
- singing a song such as "Let's all do a little listening, let's all do a little listening, let's all do a little listening, and do it right now" (to the tune of "We Wish You a Merry Christmas")
- turning off the lights and then whispering, "I see that _____ is listening, and _____ is listening," stating children's names as they turn their attention to the teacher

Once a teacher has almost all of the children's attention, he announces the need for a class meeting and gathers children where such a discussion can take place most easily (that may be gathered right around the teacher or it may be on the rug where large-group times are held). The discussion then continues with the teacher or the children involved telling about the problem and children contributing ideas and solutions.

Signals for gaining children's attention are another way to add inherent structure to playtimes. The goal is to sustain children's engagement in their play, not to interrupt it. Such signals are used only for important reasons, such as when problems arise in the classroom that need whole group attention or when other significant issues must be addressed with the whole group, such as an upcoming fire drill, a change in the schedule, or opening another area for play. Giving children opportunities to practice responding to the signals makes the signals even more important and will make the interruption time shorter because children will quiet down more quickly. They will see the respect that is demonstrated for their play experiences and be willing to give their attention briefly to matters at hand.

Allow Enough Time for Deep Play to Develop

Deep play does not develop in a short period of time. Preschool and kindergarten children need to settle into the area, consider the materials, and look at what others are doing. If they are interested in cooperative play experiences, they have to determine whose ideas they will follow and how they will work together to do so. Discussion, negotiation, and compromise will be involved. They have to try things out and see if they work. If not, problem solving will be required. Trial and error are common ways that children learn to build taller structures, connect puzzle pieces, make marble runs work, or try out new roles in dramatic play. And trial and error takes time.

> Letting the children figure out how long they want to stay with specific activities is another way of providing choice. Timing the children and making them rotate to different learning areas does not allow them the opportunity to make a plan and stick with it through completion. Adult agendas of "fifteen minutes at a center" limit children's engagement from an outside source. Many preschoolers are perfectly capable of staying with one activity for much longer than fifteen minutes, provided it is a self-chosen activity that really interests the child. When teachers remember that such engagement is an important learning goal for this age group, they can relax and not worry about the children not getting to every learning area each day. Instead, they can wonder at the intensity of a serious block builder who works cooperatively with friends over long periods of time and creates interesting structures that include symmetry and gravity-defying balance. Or they can marvel at the engagement of a socializer who spends many hours cooking and developing family scenarios in the dramatic play center. (Gronlund 2003, 90)

The structure of the daily schedule of a half-day preschool program should include at least forty-five minutes to an hour of uninterrupted playtime indoors and a separate outdoor playtime as well. (For full-day programs, both of these playtimes should be offered again in the afternoon.) So many children's lives are hectic and over-scheduled outside of their school experiences—they are rushed here and there for special activities, sports, child care, and family errands. An hour at their school to explore materials and create play scenarios may very well be the only such hour in a child's day.

Whether it is called Investigation Time, Exploration Time, Activity Time, or Choice Time, the indoor playtime is devoted to children engaged in primarily self-directed activities. If adults do interrupt, such interruptions are done respectfully and for important reasons. Otherwise, teachers provide support in order to facilitate children's attention span to grow longer and for their play to grow richer and more rewarding. When such time is given to play, children move into flow experiences and stretch their skills and abilities as they imagine and create.

This means that teachers do not schedule teacher-led small group experiences during playtime. In some programs, the children are engaged in play and the teachers call them away to join them and other children in an academically oriented task. By doing so, teachers are communicating several messages:

- My small group is more important than your play.
- My job as a teacher is to lead activities only—not to facilitate play.
- I don't value how involved you are in what you are doing—when I call you to come to small group, you must leave your play situation immediately.

Eventually, children in classrooms where play is interrupted in this manner may not invest as fully in their play experiences. They are wary of potential interruptions, watching the teachers carefully to see if they will be called away from their role plays, constructions, and investigations at the sensory table. There is nothing wrong with conducting teacher-led small groups at a different time of the day. But to bring about high-level play, teachers must provide uninterrupted, unhurried time for play in the daily schedule. By doing so they are communicating that the children's play is valued and important. They are "returning time and space for play, story, and the imagination to a secure place on the curricular shelves" (Genishi and Dyson 2009, 80).

The preschool and kindergarten classrooms of today are filled with children of diverse backgrounds, whether differing linguistically, culturally, or experientially. They need unhurried time to learn about each other, to figure out ways to enter play, and to socialize and communicate with other children in the process. There is a "cultural universal of play as a means for entering into a shared social life with other children. . . . But to do so, they require time, space, interactional partners, engaging objects, and observant teachers who both further and document the communicative strengths revealed and nurtured by play" (Genishi and Dyson 2009, 64). Time to get deeply involved is truly a gift teachers can give to young children.

> When in doubt, trust the play. It is the children's curriculum. Play that is scattered or potentially disruptive may require refocusing, but well-focused, complex play requires no intervention. . . .

Adults who interrupt play, whatever their reasons, are usually in so much of a hurry that they fail to pay attention to children's purposes. SLOW DOWN is advice to keep in mind. We shortchange young children when we hurry them. We learn most about them, and help them learn most, when we pay attention to what is happening for them as they play. (Jones and Reynolds 1992, 55–56)

The goal of play periods in preschool and kindergarten classrooms is for children to get deeply involved in high-level play. When teachers provide structure for choices, procedures for play areas, and signals to get children's attention, they will see this happen more frequently. And, they need to provide enough time for rich play to develop. Too often, children are interrupted just as soon as they get going in an exciting and interesting play scenario. The next chapter goes beyond setting up conditions, environment, and structure and looks at many actions, interventions, and techniques that teachers can use to enhance children's play.

CHAPTER 5

Interacting with Children to Enhance Play

> The play-based approach calls for teachers to know each child well and to differentiate the teaching methods to meet individual needs. It is the antithesis of the one-size-fits-all model of education. (Miller and Almon 2009, 5)

Ruby and Andre are a teaching team in a preschool classroom. They value children's play as an important and central part of their curriculum and allow up to one hour for it in the morning and in the afternoon in their daily schedule. During Choice Time, as they call it, the two of them circulate around the room, sometimes observing, sometimes helping to get a play scenario going, sometimes getting materials for another group, and sometimes joining in the play. They do not try to run small-group activities during Choice Time. They do that at a different time in the schedule. They believe strongly that they need to be available to facilitate and enhance children's play in any way they can. They learn so much about the children by watching and participating in their play. Each day as they reflect back on the day, they can share what they are learning and figure out the best strategies to help children have the best possible play experiences.

In this chapter, the focus is on the actions that teachers can take so that children's play reaches high levels. Teachers combine these actions in a variety of ways depending on their knowledge of the individual children involved, their goals at that particular moment, and the responses of the children to their interventions.

Good preschool and kindergarten teachers enhance and sustain children's high-level play by

- getting play started
- knowing when to enter and exit the play
- sustaining play through well-timed interventions
- coaching and mentoring players
- being intentional in all that they do

In using these actions, teachers are recognizing that children have an inherent drive toward mastery. They engage them in ways that challenge children's thinking and provide the support and scaffolding they need to be successful.

> Human beings, especially children, are motivated to understand or do what is just beyond their current understanding or mastery. Effective teachers create a rich learning environment to activate that motivation, and they make use of strategies to promote children's undertaking and mastering of new and progressively more advanced challenges. (Copple and Bredekamp 2009, 15)

Rather than working against the very nature of young children, teachers using these methods are instead working with it. Children enjoy play and love a challenge. By thinking in those terms, teachers can use any of the techniques in this chapter to enrich the play experiences of the children in their programs.

Productive, high-level play does not evolve in a vacuum—teachers' actions are important to its development, sustenance, and depth. As discussed in previous chapters, teachers first set up the conditions for mature play. By providing a carefully planned environment and an inherent structure, teachers communicate to children that they can take risks and be creative as they play with interesting materials and interact with each other. However, setting up these conditions is not enough. In addition, teachers must interact with children in order to facilitate their use of the environment, to help them satisfy the lower needs identified by Maslow, and to help them build their play skills and experience the flow of high-level play.

Read the following play incident and think about ways that a teacher could interact with these boys so that their play does not deteriorate into an out-of-control experience.

Three four-year-old boys are invited by their teacher to sort colored bears into round sorting trays with multiple compartments. As long as the teacher is there with them, the boys cooperate in the sorting activity, talking about the colors of the bears as they sort them. As she moves on after five or six minutes to help in another area of the classroom, their interaction with the bears changes. "Hey, I know," says Alec. "Let's see who can throw them into the tray!" The boys move the trays to the opposite end of the table and begin to throw the bears. Their initial throws involve aiming at the small compartments. As bears fly across the table and land in the compartments, some of them bounce out again onto the table from the force of the throw. The boys laugh hysterically and continue to throw the bears harder and harder. Their laughter grows louder by the minute. Soon, bears are flying across the table and onto the floor. The boys' laughter is high-pitched. They pound on and lie across the table as each bear lands. (Gronlund and James 2008, 50)

An observant teacher who heard the louder voices and hysterical laughing and saw the boys' wilder actions would immediately move across the room to interact and intervene. How the teacher chooses to intervene is the question. Are there ways to help the boys regain control and become more interested and engaged in working with these materials? Are they showing that they have lost interest in the original sorting task and need more challenge in order to be fully engaged? Although one option is always to suggest that the materials be put away and the boys play elsewhere, the teacher may find that reaction extreme and not necessary. In fact, this is seldom the best response and should be the one of last resort.

Instead, the teacher may be able to help the boys settle down by introducing different ways to use the colored bears, challenging them to make different kinds of patterns or to measure the length of the table in colored bears. Or she may determine that throwing things is their real interest and offer them beanbags or soft balls to throw at targets outdoors or in another part of the classroom. Teachers can choose from many options when facilitating children's play. Chaotic or simplistic play can usually be changed when an adult intervenes in a way that will enhance the play experience so the children can sustain their engagement in a positive and productive manner.

Intentional Teaching

One of the important tenets of developmentally appropriate practice is the intentionality of the teacher. In early childhood programs, especially those for preschoolers, curriculum is often an integration of many approaches and many ways to use materials. Even in kindergarten classrooms with more defined curricular approaches, the changing nature of the children's interests and levels of engagement can be challenging. That's why it's so important that teachers really think about what they are doing. Being a reflective practitioner is essential for early childhood professionals.

> Good teachers continually use their knowledge and judgment to make intentional decisions about which materials, interactions, and learning experiences are likely to be most effective for the group and for each individual child in it . . .
>
> An effective teacher makes use of the strategy that fits a particular situation and the purpose or purposes she has in mind. . . . She has a variety of strategies at the ready and remains flexible and observant so that she can determine which to use. (Copple and Bredekamp 2009, 36)

Teacher intentionality is not just important when leading small and large groups, planning for field trips and special visitors, or gathering assessment information. Intentionality and play go together too. The process of supporting and sustaining children's play engagement is a complex one. There are many ways to interact with children, depending on the needs of the moment. Teachers must observe children as they play and then make on-the-spot decisions about what actions to take with them. They are continually analyzing the play situation and trying out different approaches with the children. They also may plan for interventions in children's play and see how they work. Good teachers are making hundreds of decisions each day, continually assessing situations and thinking: What's the best way for me to help this child or this group of children right now? As the following graphic shows, this process is an ongoing cycle of actions, including observing, reflecting, making plans, and trying things out.

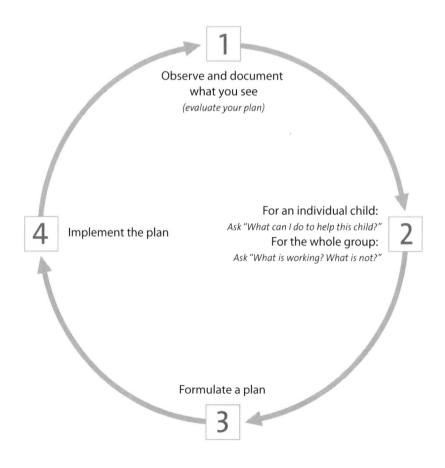

1

Observe and document
what you see
(evaluate your plan)

For an individual child:
Ask "What can I do to help this child?"
For the whole group:
Ask "What is working? What is not?"

2

4 Implement the plan

Formulate a plan

3

As teachers engage in this reflective practice, they try out a variety of teaching strategies to promote high-level play. The following list is adapted from the new edition of DAP (Copple and Bredekamp 2009, 36–37) and identifies a number of possibilities. It also includes comments a teacher could make when supporting children's play.

- Acknowledge what the children are doing or saying.
  "Wow, I see that you all built a garage for your trucks. It's got very high walls. You stacked lots of long blocks up to make those walls."

- Encourage their efforts.
  "Your grocery store sure is a busy place. You have customers who are shopping and a cashier at the checkout. Oh, and you're stocking the shelves!"

- Give specific feedback.
  "You have spent a long time on your Lego construction. I see you put wheels on your vehicle and you have some people riding in it. Where are they going?"

- Model attitudes, problem solving, and behavior toward others.
  "Sometimes, I can't figure out what to make with my playdough. So, I just roll it and roll it, and pound it, and feel it with my fingers. I don't always have to make something, do I?"

- Demonstrate to show the correct way to do something.
  "If you want the water wheel to go around when you pour the water into it, you have to pull open the latch at the bottom like this. There! Then, it works."

- Create or add challenge.
  "I wonder if you could build something with all of the blocks?"

- Ask questions that provoke children's thinking.
  "What do you think would happen if we put water on the sand? How would it change? Would we need some different tools to work with it?"

- Offer assistance.
  "Would you like some help getting the marble run to stop toppling over? Maybe if we made stronger foundations with some of the pieces, it would stay up. I'll help you do that."

- Provide information.

  "You made an ambulance with your Duplos. Remember when we saw the ambulance that came to our school? The EMTs had a special bed on wheels, didn't they? That was called a stretcher."

- Give directions.

  "We have lots of art materials for you to play and create with at the art table. You may use glue or paste to make whatever kind of collage you can think of."

Teachers use these strategies alone and in combination. They use them in every activity of the day as they interact with children. They think about which strategies will work best to help the children be more productive and engaged in sustained, high-level play. Here is a look at some other actions teachers can take to support and enhance children's play.

How to Get Play Started

Sometimes teachers have to get play started. They may notice children who are wandering around the classroom or outdoor area aimlessly, not settling into any activity. A teacher may approach a wandering child and ask her what she would like to do. If the child doesn't have any ideas of her own, the teacher may make several suggestions. Or the teacher may take a wandering child by the hand, lead him over to an established play scenario, and help him join in by providing the language needed to join in social interaction with the other children and modeling what can be done with the play materials. For example, the teacher might say: "Hey, I see that you are making lots of interesting things with your playdough. May Andrew and I join you? Gee, Andrew, what should we make? Shall we make a bird's nest with some tiny eggs like Monica's or some long, squiggly snakes like Jack is making? Jack, can you show Andrew how to make those? What do you have to do?"

If teachers see instances of chaotic or simplistic play that need their attention, they may need to help more productive play get started. Dramatic play that is merely imitative of the most popular cartoon show of the day will usually remain at the simplistic level and be unsatisfying for the children. In that case, teachers may need to help get a different play theme going. They may present different character ideas. For example, they might ask: "Do you think the bad guy likes kittens? He'd have to take care of his kitty, wouldn't he? How can we help him do that?" Or they may suggest that a different theme be played altogether: "How about if we start a restaurant to cook the food for some kings and queens?" Teachers pay close attention to the children's responses. If the questions or suggestions do not spark their interest, the teacher tries others until something does. When children respond positively to an idea, teachers help them follow through with getting the necessary materials and setting up the play scenario. Sometimes they are successful in getting new, more complex play started and sometimes not. If not, teachers will have to take some of the other steps that will be identified throughout this chapter.

Over time, teachers may reflect on how things are going in playtimes for their group of children and determine that they would like to try to start a new play theme or idea. They may decide that the children are ready for a change in their experiences, or notice that the children are showing some interest in a particular play theme or set of materials. Or it may be that the teacher has new materials or ideas to introduce to them. Consider the following play story:

Outdoor Dramatic Play—Airplanes

At the end of the day, Janet talked with her colleague, Laurene, about their prekindergarten students. Janet said, "Have you noticed that children don't really use our dramatic play area outdoors?" The area had two small playhouses and a plastic workbench. The two discussed ways to get play going in this area and decided that the next day they would provide some new dress-up clothes that included hats and jackets for a variety of jobs, including airline pilot, police officer, firefighter, and construction worker. Janet finished their conversation, saying, "Let's try it and see what happens."

The next day, before going outdoors, Janet announced to the children, "We have some new things for you to play with outdoors. We have new hats and jackets that you might be interested in wearing in our dramatic play area outside. Come over there if you're interested." Seven children followed Janet out the door and helped her open the packages. Ooh's and ah's were heard as children took turns trying on the firefighter hat, the police jacket, and the construction worker's vest and hard hat. Michael put on the pilot's hat and announced to the group, "Let's make an airplane! I'm the pilot, I'll fly it." He dragged a chair out of the playhouse and put it next to the plastic workbench. "Here are my controls. Hurry up everybody. We're going to take off." Children wearing the other costumes looked at each other and at Michael, but did not move. "How about we get some more chairs from the classroom to be your seats on the airplane?" Janet asked. Six volunteers immediately jumped to the task. Chairs were brought out and set up behind Michael. "Wait a minute," José said. "You need a copilot to help you drive the plane." José put on the police hat, placed a chair next to Michael, and said, "There. I'll be your helper." Children sat in the other chairs and talked about where they were going. "Africa," said Renee. "No, New York," said Tanikah. Janet suggested that maybe the plane could go to lots of different places. This seemed to satisfy the girls. Some of the passengers were still wearing the hats or jackets; others were not. The play continued for approximately ten minutes with various children taking turns being the pilot and copilot. Michael and José willingly gave up their hats and seats, and joined the other passengers as the plane took off for Africa, New York, and Disney World.

Janet and Laurene started a new play endeavor and the children took it over for themselves. This is a critical consideration in getting play started—teachers can provide materials (the hats and jackets) and facilitation (chairs for airplane seats), but they still recognize that the ownership of the play and its story line are up to the children. Their goal is to get children's imaginations going and then to be ready to facilitate further, if necessary. Michael's idea of pilots and airplanes was his alone, not suggested by Janet or Laurene. And the other children went along with that play scenario, participating as copilots and passengers.

Know When to Enter and Exit the Play

Once the play is started, a teacher has to pay close attention to the children's cues to know when to enter or exit the play. Janet and Laurene wisely stayed out of the airplane play once it got going. They remained nearby, observing to see if the rotating roles of different pilots and passengers were working for the group. When they saw that they were, they felt confident that the children could sustain this role-play experience. And the children did so for ten minutes. However, soon after that, Laurene realized that she needed to enter the play to help the children. Here's what happened:

Outdoor Dramatic Play—Airplanes (continued)

When Michael and José had been pilot and copilot, respectively, they called out to the other children to fasten seat belts, get ready for takeoff, and prepare for landing. Michael, especially, provided suggestions for actions for the passengers to follow and they did. As the players changed their roles and different children took on the pilot and copilot positions, the nature of the play changed. Some pilots merely drove the plane and did not talk to the passengers. Some pilots gave stern reprimands to the passengers to sit down and be quiet. The children sitting in the passenger chairs became restless and some left the play. Laurene observed all of this and wondered to herself if there was something she could do to enhance the situation.

She decided to get slips of paper and markers and pulled over a small table next to the "airplane" (chairs and workbench). "Do you all have your tickets for this flight?" she asked as she sat down at the table, the construction worker's hard hat on her head. "I'm the ticket counter lady. You better come get your tickets so you can go on the airplane." The passengers jumped up from their seats and gathered around her. "You can make your own tickets, if you want," Laurene suggested. Some children made markings or wrote their names on the tickets, while others wrote numbers designating a flight number. Jessica, a girl who was wearing the construction worker's vest, announced, "Hey everybody, I'm the ticket taker. You have to give me your tickets before you get on the plane." As each child handed a ticket to her, she looked at it carefully and said, "You're in number one. You're in number two," and so on. Timothy, who was wearing the pilot's hat, asked Jessica, "Do you have all the tickets?" When Jessica nodded her head, he called out, "Put on your seat belts everybody. Let's blast off." He counted from one to ten before blasting off. The passengers responded by pretending to fasten seat belts, holding on to their chairs, and counting along with him.

The ticket making and taking scenario continued and the plane "took off and landed" several more times, again with a rotation in the children acting as pilots. Jessica remained the ticket taker throughout, but also took on the role of creating tickets for any new children who joined as passengers. Laurene provided more chairs so that the plane could accommodate everyone, but otherwise exited the play again, staying nearby in case she was needed. The play continued in this manner for another twenty-five minutes.

Once play is started and children are engaged, teachers must still be observant. Laurene noticed that Michael's ideas had helped the other children define their roles and stay interested in being passengers. But as other children played the pilot role, they did not give such directions and passengers started leaving the play. Laurene saw this and decided to step in and create a new role—providing tickets. Her involvement was needed only for a very brief time because Jessica followed up with a new role of her own—ticket taker. Thus, a whole new aspect of the play developed and children's passenger play had more complexity and purpose. Then, Timothy introduced the "blast off" process (confusing airplanes with rocket ships), which gave the passengers another way to be more involved in the scene. Again, wisely, Laurene exited the play and let the children continue on their own, providing more chairs so other children could join in, but staying out of the actual play scenario.

Effective teachers engage in a careful process of stepping in and out of children's play. This process is much like dancing with a partner, where one leads and the other follows. Teachers watch the play to determine if the children have the lead and are being successful in furthering the play scenario, or if they need them to step in and take the lead for a short time to help enhance or complicate the play. But teachers quickly step out again, turning the lead back over to the children. Teachers value the creative problem solving that self-directed play can require, and they want to empower the children to engage in cooperative negotiation of roles and determination of story lines as much as possible.

Determining when to enter or exit children's play comes with experience in reading children's cues and signals. It may be helpful for teachers to enter children's play when they see the following:

- children repeating the same actions again and again
- children getting frustrated in trying to negotiate roles and responsibilities with each other
- players leaving the area with fewer remaining to try to sustain the play

Teachers may find that they are more successful in entering play if they do so within the script the children are playing as Laurene did. By doing so, Laurene was validating the play scenario and encouraging the children to keep it going. Even when entering play in order to provide a safety element, a teacher can use the language of the children's scenario when giving a friendly reminder about use of materials.

Block Play

Three boys have been building with wooden blocks for most of Choice Time. Jesse says, "Hey, it's a castle and Voldemort is coming. He's the bad, bad guy and Harry Potter has to fight him!" Jesse has led the action as Philip and Andre have constructed the castle. The teacher, Tanya, has noticed that the play has gotten louder and louder as the castle has grown in size. "Watch out!" Jesse yells and throws himself down on the ground, knocking down part of the castle wall. "Hey!" Andre yells. "Jesse, you knocked down my wall." Tanya moves over to the block area and quietly says, "Hey, Gryffindors, be careful over here. You won't be able to fight off Lord Voldemort if you don't have a strong castle wall." Jesse jumps up and says, "Come on, Gryffindors, let's build this up again before the bad guys come to get Harry Potter." Tanya moves away as the boys return to their construction task more quietly and with focus.

Children want to sustain their play. "Children's eagerness to stay in the play situation motivates them to attend to and operate within its structure, conforming to what is required by the other players and by the play scenario" (Copple and Bredekamp 2009, 131). Teachers can work with this desire by entering the play in ways that will keep children involved, resolve the problem that has arisen, and get them back into the flow of the play action.

Exiting the play is important as well and requires teachers to be very sensitive to the children's cues to know when to exit. In the block play scenario

above, Tanya saw that her friendly reminder (phrased in the language of the Harry Potter books) led the boys to resume building in a quieter and more constructive manner. She could let them continue, independent of her direct involvement. Of course, she still watched closely to see if they were successful. However, sometimes adults overstay their welcome in a play scenario. They enter the children's play with the best of intentions, but do not time their exit well. When teachers stay involved in children's play for too long, they may inadvertently take over the play scenario. The children grow dependent on the teacher's suggestions, ideas, or external control. Teachers must be continually asking themselves: "Are the children taking ownership of this play? Are they contributing their own ideas and suggestions or are they merely following mine?" If the latter is true, the children may have slipped back from high level to simplistic play. Consider the following play scenario. Does the teacher read the children's cues that it is time to exit the play?

Outdoor Sand Play

Two four-year-old girls were playing outside on a beautiful, sunny, spring day. They had taken off their shoes and were using small, plastic shovels to dig in the sand around the climbing structure. Some of the sand covered Anna's feet. "Oh!" she cried out. "That sand is really cool on my toes." "I know," said Kendra. "Let's dig a hole and cover our feet with sand." They proceeded to do so, laughing and talking as they dug the hole, stuck in their feet, and filled the hole up to their shins. A student teacher, Matt, came by and asked, "Hey girls, what happened to your feet?" "We covered them up with the sand!" the girls replied, giggling. "But where are your toes?" Matt asked. The girls wiggled their toes and sand fell away until their feet were visible again. "Do you want me to cover them up again?" Matt asked. "Yes!" was the enthusiastic reply. By then, two other children had joined. They took off their shoes and shouted to Matt, "Cover mine! Cover mine!" Matt obliged and ended up with a group of six children sitting in a circle, demanding that he cover their feet with sand. Matt worked hard, digging sand and pouring it over the children's feet while the children sat back, calling out, "More, Matt, more!" and waiting while he tried to meet their demands.

Matt meant well in joining the children's play. He asked what they were doing, encouraging them to talk about their play, his interest validating their engagement. However, he took over the play instead of enhancing it. The children became passive recipients dependent on his actions. They were not contributing ideas or problem solving in any way. Like Matt, many teachers find themselves in situations where their involvement in the children's play does not enhance it. It's important to recognize this and turn the play back over to the children.

Here is a list of signals that indicate it is time to exit the play:

- children become passively involved rather than active participants in creating the play situation
- children become louder, more demanding, and more out of control
- children ignore the teacher's suggestions and continue doing what they were doing
- children leave the play area

What could Matt have done differently? There are ways to exit play that enhance it for children. Here's what Matt did:

Outdoor Sand Play, continued

Matt realizes that the children are getting louder and more strident as they yell out. He sees that he's doing all of the work and that the children are in a passive role. "Hey everybody," he says as he stops digging. "How about if we get more shovels so everybody can do some digging and covering up feet? I need help! This is too much for just me to do." Three of the children pull their feet out of the sand and go to get shovels. The other three wait for them to return. When they do, Matt says, "How about we take turns? Some of you can be the diggers and cover the others' feet. Then, we'll switch." The children agree to this division of labor and play it out while Matt sits off to the side giving encouragement but no longer doing the digging himself. The children stay engaged for another ten to fifteen minutes.

It's important for preschool and kindergarten teachers to keep in mind that the goal is for children to direct their own play as much as possible. "When you intentionally involve yourself in play to further children's cognitive skills, interactions with peers, or role playing, you scaffold the learning so they can reach their optimal development. As children reach that development, adults move back and let children carry the play" (Heidemann and Hewitt 2010, 116). Adult interaction and support may very well be needed. But the play has more value when adults provide just the right amount of support so that it can be sustained by the children, not dependent on the adult to lead every aspect of it and not placing children in passive roles. "Children who are capable of directing their own play often just leave or become uninterested when the adult is too involved in forming the play scenario" (Heidemann and Hewitt 2010, 117). Knowing when to enter and exit play takes careful observation of the play as it is occurring and consideration of the children's response when an adult does enter the play.

Sustain Play through Well-Timed Interventions

Like entering and exiting play, teachers also have to be careful in using questions and comments as a way to enhance children's play. Sometimes a teacher's best intentions when interacting with children in play actually interrupt what is happening. The goal is to facilitate the play, to help it move to or sustain a higher level. Unfortunately, some teachers think that in order to incorporate early learning standards and curricular goals into play experiences, they need to interrupt what the children are doing to ask questions about concepts. For example, they may ask, "How many medium-sized bears do you have?" or "What color is that plate?" This is just not the case. There are ways to integrate standards and goals into play that do not interrupt. Chapter 8 explores effective integration strategies in more depth.

In the following example of a teacher's involvement with children in a dramatic play scenario, is the teacher helping the children sustain their engagement or is she interrupting what they are doing?

Magic Capes

Three boys and one girl (all four-year-olds) are playing in the dramatic play area, putting scarves around their backs and calling them "magic capes." Ms. Denise helps them tie the scarves and asks them, "Why are the scarves magic?" Jacob responds, "Because they make us fly!" and proceeds to laugh loudly and run around the room. Eli and Luis follow him, bumping into each other, while Alejandra watches quietly. Ms. Denise says, "If you boys don't settle down, we'll have to take the scarves away. Why don't you come over here and play with Alejandra? I know! Your magic capes could be magic chef capes to help you cook a wonderful dinner." The boys continue to run around the room and Alejandra remains where she is. (Gronlund and James 2008, 56)

The timing of questions or comments is important. Well-timed questions can encourage children to think, problem solve, try a different approach, incorporate symbolic materials, or develop new play themes. If done well, the results should be evident: the children show greater interest in their play; they complicate what they are doing; and they sustain their engagement for longer periods. However, poorly timed questioning can turn children off to the play altogether. It's an interruption. It stops the flow of the play. It makes the children lose their investment in the roles they were playing or in the construction process they were enjoying. "Even when the teacher is asking the children to tell her what to do, she is still directing the play, although subtly, and thus play is now a teacher-directed activity" (Bodrova and Leong 2007, 146). Teacher-directed activities do not give children the opportunity to develop their own self-regulation while child-directed play does. Teachers must figure out ways to interact with children in support of their self-regulation.

How does a teacher know when to step in and ask some questions or make some comments without interrupting or directing children's play? One way is to establish a quiet presence near the play area. Instead of pushing into the play scenario, good teachers observe nearby, giving attention (and therefore value) to what's going on, but not interacting at first. Instead, they watch and listen. Then, they may begin with comments that acknowledge or encourage what the children are doing. For example, a teacher might say something like, "Boy, I see lots of cooks in that kitchen!" Or, "You children are sure working together to build that ramp. It's really long!" If the children ignore the comments, the teacher may decide to observe a bit longer. But if the children respond, the teacher has an invitation to enter into the play with a question or two.

If children call teachers over to their play area and invite them to see what they've done, they are giving the teacher an opportunity to make comments and ask questions as well. Children delight in sharing their constructions, successes, and story lines with the caring adults in their lives. Their play is important to them. So, when teachers are responsive to their invitations to see what they are doing, they can take advantage of a great opportunity to interact in ways that will enhance the play even more. Here's an example of a teacher who established a quiet presence nearby and then was invited into a child's pretend scenario.

Going to the Moon

Enrique had turned the workbench into a spaceship. After he played for a few minutes he said, "Ms. Donna, pretend you are my boss." Ms. Donna said, "Okay." He said, "Boss?" Ms. Donna said, "Yes?" He said, "How do we get to the moon?" Ms. Donna said, "Go two degrees south then forty-three degrees west." He said, "Okay, here we go. Put your seat belt on. Three, two, one. Blast off." After a minute or two he said, "We're coming in for a landing. Oh no, we're going to crash!" After the crash he asked, "Are you okay, Boss?" Ms. Donna said, "Yes!" He said, "Good. Do you know we only had five seconds of fuel left when we landed?"

When the timing is right, what kinds of questions should teachers ask? Open-ended questions are usually better. Close-ended questions have only one answer and include questions like

- How many do you have?
- What color or shape is this?
- Which piece matches?
- What letter is this?

Open-ended questions, on the other hand, have many possible answers. They encourage thinking, problem solving, and applying knowledge. They challenge children to figure things out themselves while the teacher gently guides them toward a successful solution or an interesting discovery. Vygotskians call this "educational dialogue," and compare it to the questioning techniques used by the Greek philosopher Socrates. "The teacher has a goal in mind and uses questions to guide the students toward that goal" (Bodrova and Leong 2007, 85). Here are some examples of open-ended questions and prompts:

- What do you think will happen if you . . . ?
- Tell me about your construction or creation.
- What's going on in your house (hospital, restaurant, spaceship)?
- What else could happen in your house (hospital, restaurant, spaceship)?
- Do you need something else to make that construction (play house)?
- What ideas do you have to solve that problem?

Teachers learn a lot about children's thinking when they ask such questions. They may uncover misunderstandings about how something works or miscommunications among the players in the scenario. They can see where support is needed, where additional materials might be helpful, or where some mediation could take place.

And what kinds of comments sustain children's play rather than interrupt it? Comments that acknowledge and encourage rather than praise and compliment sustain play. Instead of saying "Good job," or "You look so pretty in your dress-up clothes," a teacher says, "Wow, you used lots of blocks to build that bridge," or "I see that you're wearing a hat and high-heeled shoes." Then the teacher can follow up with questions that will get the child thinking, such as, "What else might you need to add to your bridge? Does it need more support anywhere? Are there other details that you might include?" and "Who are you pretending to be when you are all dressed up like that? Where are you going? Someplace special? What will you do there?" The combination of encouraging comments and open-ended questions sustain children's engagement rather than interrupting it in most circumstances.

Consider the following scenario. Are the teacher's questions and comments well-timed and do they help to facilitate the children's play?

Lego Constructions Scene #1

Three four-year-olds had been working at the Lego table for ten minutes, each building vehicles with wheels, when the teacher, Anita, sat down and said, "Hey, you guys, what kind of cars are you building?" Latisha said, "It's an ambulance." Marco said nothing, as did Tony. "How many wheels on your ambulance?" Anita asked. Latisha replied, "I'm still building it. It's gonna rescue people in the accidents." Marco picked up his construction and flew it in the air, making an engine noise as he did so. Anita asked, "What kind of airplane did you make, Marco?" "It's not an airplane—it's the space shuttle," he replied. "Oh, what colors of Legos did you use on your shuttle?" Marco flew his space shuttle over to the block area leaving the Lego table altogether. Throughout all of this conversation, Tony continued to work quietly, putting more Legos together for a very long vehicle. Anita said, "Tony, what are you making?" Tony whispered, "My grandma and grandpa's got one." "They have a big car like that?" she asked. Tony responded, "No, they go camping in it and they park it in my driveway when they come visit." "Oh, is it an RV or a trailer?" Anita said. "I sometimes sleep in it when they come," he said. She asked, "How many people can sleep in it?" Tony said, "Sometimes we cook in it too."

Anita's intentions were good ones, but her questioning was an interruption to the children's play. She did not establish a quiet presence nearby their play and was not invited to join them. In her first approach, she assumed the children were making cars without asking about their constructions. She asked mostly close-ended questions and did not follow up on what the children told her to engage in a supportive dialogue with them. They gave her hints about their understanding of ambulances, space shuttles, and recreational vehicles.

But instead of following up on those topics, she continued to return to questions about how many and what colors were involved. Consider the scene again with Anita attempting to sustain the children's play using a different approach:

Lego Constructions Scene #2

Three four-year-olds had been working at the Lego table for ten minutes, each building vehicles with wheels, while the teacher, Anita, quietly sat nearby and watched. Latisha turned to her and said, "Look, Anita. It's an ambulance." "Oh," Anita replied. "I can see it has some people on it." Marco said nothing, as did Tony. Latisha replied, "I'm still building it. It's gonna rescue people in the accidents." Anita asked, "Was there a car accident or a different kind of accident?" Latisha responded, "Yeah, some cars got crashed." Anita said, "Oh dear, what will happen when the ambulance gets to the accident?" "It's gonna take the people to the hospital," Latisha said. Marco picked up his construction and flew it in the air, making an engine noise as he did so. Anita said, "I hear your construction making a noise, Marco." "It's the space shuttle," he replied. "Where is your space shuttle flying to?" she asked. Marco flew his space shuttle over to the block area leaving the Lego table altogether. Anita said, "To the block area?" "Yeah, it's gonna land over there and then it will come back," he said. Throughout all of this conversation, Tony continued to work quietly putting more Legos together for a very long vehicle. "Tony, I see that your vehicle is really long," Anita said. Tony whispered, "My grandma and grandpa's got one." "They do, huh?" Anita replied. He said, "Yeah, they go camping in it and they park it in my driveway when they come visit." Anita asked, "Oh, like a camper with beds?" Tony said, "I sometimes sleep in it when they come." "What else can you do in the camper?" Anita asked. And Tony said, "Sometimes we cook in it too." Anita said, "I wonder if there's a way that you could make the kitchen in your Lego camper. Do you see any Legos that might help you? What could you use for a table or for the chairs?" Marco flew his space shuttle back over to the table and landed it in front of Anita. "Is your space shuttle going on another trip? Where will your space shuttle fly to next?" she asked him. The construction play continued for another twenty minutes with lots more conversation and building.

Anita did not interrupt, but established a quiet presence nearby and then waited for an invitation before engaging with the group at the table. Rather than having an agenda of goals unrelated to the children's construction play, she asked questions that encouraged the children to talk further about their constructions and think about added details.

There are some times when an interruption and a well-timed question or comment can turn the play around. If the situation needs immediate adult intervention because of safety issues, questions or comments may be a way to very quickly turn the play back to something more productive for the children. If safety is not a concern, then it may be wiser to establish a quiet presence and wait for an invitation to join in children's play before using such strategies. Remember the Throwing Bears scenario from earlier in this chapter? In that instance the play deteriorated into hilarity and throwing of objects. It could have become dangerous, chaotic, and out of control. The following story shows one way of using interrupting and questioning to turn such play around.

Throwing Colored Bears with Teacher Questioning

Three four-year-old boys are invited by their teacher, Gina, to sort colored bears into round sorting trays with multiple compartments. As long as she is there with them, the boys cooperate in the sorting activity, talking about the colors of the bears as they sort them. As she moves on after five or six minutes to help in another area of the classroom, their interaction with the bears changes. "Hey, I know," says Alec. "Let's see who can throw them into the tray!" The boys move the trays to the opposite end of the table and begin to throw the bears. Their initial throws involve aiming at the small compartments. As bears fly across the table and land in the compartments, some of them bounce out again onto the table from the force of the throw. The boys laugh hysterically and continue to throw the bears harder and harder. Their laughter grows louder by the minute. Soon, bears are flying across the table and onto the floor. The boys' laughter is high-pitched. They pound on and lie across the table as each bear lands. (Gronlund and James 2008, 50)

Gina moves across the room and says to the boys, "It's gotten very loud over here. And I see that you're throwing the bears instead of sorting them." The boys stop throwing but still giggle. She continues, "It looks to me like you wanted to do something different with the bears. That's okay. But throwing them into these small compartments probably isn't safe. What are some other things that you might do with the bears?" The boys look at her blankly, and Noah says, "I don't know." Gina says, "I wonder if you might like to practice throwing with something else, like beanbags and soft balls. We could set up a hoop as the target over there across the room. You could try throwing from different distances and see how many times you can get the beanbags and balls inside the hoop. What do you think?" Noah and his friends yell out, "Yeah! Let's do that." Gina suggests that they clean up the bears first, then help her get out the throwing items and hoop. She then supervises as they play the throwing game.

Gina made it clear that throwing the bears in the compartments was not to continue. Then she made comments about what she had seen and asked questions about the boys' interests. When she saw that they did not have any clear ideas on how to use the bears in a safe way, she suggested that they consider throwing suitable items. They responded positively to that and were able to continue playing productively after her interruption and suggestion for a new activity.

Coach and Mentor the Players

Sometimes children need a coach or mentor to be successful in play experiences. It's preferable to have a child in this mentoring role. "Other children are much more effective mentors for play than the teacher, because the child is a 'child,' which means that they can engage in play without making it a teacher-directed activity" (Bodrova and Leong 2007, 153). However, some children need the help of a teacher to enter play, to engage with others, or to sustain play. Once again, teachers are faced with that tricky balance that was discussed before—that dance where the lead keeps changing between teacher and child. The goal is to provide just the right amount of support so that children can move into play experiences on their own without the need of adult involvement.

In what ways can teachers coach or mentor a child in play? Most of the suggestions in this chapter are ways of coaching: getting play started, knowing when to enter and exit the play, and sustaining play through well-timed interventions. These strategies involve teachers briefly; they step out of the action as quickly as possible. But for some children, that's not enough. They will not move beyond chaotic or simplistic play without a teacher by their side, acting as a coplayer, modeling play behaviors, and talking through the play process. "Coplayers function as equal play partners with children. . . . The teacher carefully follows the flow of the dramatic action, letting the children take the lead most of the time. In being the children's play partner, opportunities often arise for the teacher to model sociodramatic play skills such as role playing, make-believe transformations, and peer interaction strategies" (Johnson, Christie, and Wardle 2005, 272). Acting as a coplayer can be very helpful for a child who has behavioral problems or poor social skills. Consider the following play scenario:

Doggie Play

Three kindergarten girls were playing in the house corner. Mahela was on all fours, barking and growling. Christine and Lucia were attempting to get Mahela to follow them around. "Come on, doggie. You're on your leash. You have to come this way. We're taking you for walk." No matter what they said, Mahela crawled in a different direction. Lucia called out, "I have a juicy bone. I have a juicy bone." Briefly, Mahela crawled back and pretended to gobble the bone, then took off again. Finally, Christine said, "Forget it, Lucia. Let's go cook dinner. Just leave her." The two girls went back into the kitchen area of the house corner and started to play with the pots and pans. Mahela stayed off to the side, still on all fours, panting and watching the girls.

The teacher, Phil, had been observing this scenario. He knew that Mahela did not have many established social relationships in the class and often played alone. He thought this might be a good opportunity to try to support her initial attempts to engage with the other girls—and he guessed that being the dog probably was a safer, more comfortable role for her than being herself. He pulled a chair over next to Mahela and asked, "Can I be a doggie with you?" Mahela nodded her head. Phil sat in his chair, put up his hands like paws, and panted along with Mahela. "Ruff, ruff," he said. "We doggies want some dog food, ruff, ruff." Mahela growled and nodded her head. Lucia and Christine brought over two pots and put them down in front of the doggies. Christine said, "Here you go. Here's some dog food we just made for you, doggies." Mahela and Phil pretended to eat it, then Mahela began to crawl off again. Phil said, "Ruff, ruff, now you have to take us for a walk over to the block area. Ruff, ruff, doggie Mahela, come back, we're going for our walk." Mahela watched as Phil crouched down and walked along with Lucia and Christine. "Ruff, ruff, I have my leash on so I'm walking with my masters," he said. Mahela crawled back over and joined the party. Lucia called out, "Let's find some balls to play catch with our doggies. That's what my dog does. He likes to chase tennis balls." Back in his teacher role, Phil suggested that they get the basket of soft balls down from the shelf. As he helped them get the basket, Mahela chased after a ball Lucia threw, picked it up in her mouth, and brought it back to Lucia. Phil suggested she use her paws instead to prevent germs spreading, and the girls continued to engage in a throw and fetch game for another few minutes. Then Mahela said, "Ruff, ruff, doggie go to sleep now." The girls made a dog bed of blankets, covered up Mahela, and petted her as she pretended to sleep. "I'm done playing," Mahela announced after a couple of minutes. Phil thought, "That was a pretty sustained interaction for Mahela," and smiled to himself.

When working in an inclusive setting, preschool and kindergarten teachers may find that they need to coach children with special needs as well as their typically developing peers. The play of children with special needs will be influenced by their developmental capabilities. They may need the teacher to provide entry into a playgroup and language to communicate in the play. Or they may need to imitate a teacher's actions in order to move into pretend play and may need directions for what to do. Consider this example:

Feeding the Baby

Andy, a boy with Down syndrome, attends an inclusionary preschool with typically developing peers. His teacher, Ellen, is working on engaging Andy and his peers in play together. Today she sees that several children are playing family roles in the dramatic play area— cooking, washing dishes, and caring for babies. She invites Andy to join her in that area and he agrees. "Hi, Mom and Dad," Ellen says. "The big brother and sister are here to help take care of the babies." Joseph looks up from the stove, "Are you the sister, Miss Ellen?" "I am," she replies, "and Andy's the big brother. Do you want us to give the babies their bottles?" "Sure," Joseph replies. Marissa brings over the bottles and says, "Here you go. I'm the Mom, but I'm going shopping. So you guys got to babysit, okay?" Ellen gets a baby and holds it gently in her arms, feeding it the bottle. "See, Andy? Can you get a baby and feed it too?" Andy imitates her actions and smiles broadly.

Coplaying can also be a way to encourage typically developing children to include children with special needs in the play experience.

The way that the teacher structures the classroom can support children's interactions. For example, researchers reported increased peer interaction between children with and without disabilities when teachers introduced activities, established rules, assigned roles, and provided materials. . . .

Activities that were more structured required fewer social skills for children to interact, and better allowed for children with and without disabilities to participate together. . . .

Teachers not only manipulate the environment to provide various types of activities for children, but they also model appropriate social interactions and facilitate social interactions between children with and without disabilities. . . . Play behavior between children with and without disabilities may be initiated by teachers, and children's continued interaction may be further supported by teachers." (Hestenes and Carroll 2000, 232)

When coaching children in play and becoming a coplayer with them, teachers do not need to focus on dramatic play alone. Teachers can also join in block building, construction with manipulatives, and sensory play. Modeling how to use the materials in different ways, and providing a steady verbal stream of "think talk" can help the children complicate what they are doing as in the following scenario:

Block Play with the Teacher

Preschool teacher Alana had noticed that the block play going on in her classroom was repetitive and lackluster. Children stacked blocks and compared sizes, but they did not coordinate their actions with each other, nor did they describe what they were building (a restaurant, fort, or bridge). So Alana decided to join the block builders today and announced this as children were choosing their play activities at large-group time. "Today, I'm going to be one of the people building in the block area," Alana announced. "I really like to build with blocks. Hmmm, I wonder what I'll build? I'll have to think about that and make a plan." The children laughed and clamored for who would join her. She helped them make their choices and assured everyone who was interested that they would get a chance throughout the day to work with her in blocks.

In the block area, Alana kept up a running conversation with herself, describing her actions, sharing her thinking, and wondering aloud what she might add next as she placed block after block on her structure. Children built alongside of her, listening and sometimes making suggestions, or adding something to her structure. As they did so, Alana asked, "Would you like to build with me? We could make this much better together, don't you think?" Soon she had all of the children working together with her on a large, extensive structure. "What do you think we're making here?" she asked. Several ideas were shared and they took a vote—a McDonald's restaurant. "If it's McDonald's, where are the golden arches?" Alana asked. One child found arches. Another child decided to make the sign and got paper, markers, and tape. Other children went off to the house area to bring back food items to sell in the McDonald's. Before long, hamburgers and fries were being sold and the scene had changed into both construction and dramatic play. Alana became more and more quiet as the children took over the play, her running commentary no longer needed.

There are many actions that teachers can take to enhance children's play so that it reaches this high level. This chapter has identified several of them. The next chapter takes the idea of teacher facilitation to another level and looks at provocations and emotions as powerful ways to lead preschoolers and kinder-gartners to even more rewarding and beneficial play.

CHAPTER 6

Provoking Children into More Complex Play

> The interventions are careful and specific—designed to facilitate children's thinking, to "provoke" them to go further in their thinking. . . . Rather than constraining children, the teachers are seeking to open up the possibilities for them, just as a maestro helps students learn to play an instrument, but does not make the music for them. (Kantor and Whaley 1998, 322)

Gail and Mark had both noticed over the past couple of weeks that their class of kindergarten children was not making good use of the dramatic play area. Much of the play involved taking all of the plastic food items, dishes, and silverware and dumping them on the table. No scripts developed for the play. The children were often silly and loud. Both teachers had tried a variety of interventions to get more productive play going without positive results. During their Friday afternoon planning session, they decided they would do something radical to provoke a response from the children to see what might develop. Here's what happened:

Kindergarten Bakery

At the end of group meeting time on Monday morning, Gail announced, "We have something different in the dramatic play area. In fact, why don't we all go over there right now so you can see what's changed." The group followed Mark and Gail over to the corner of the classroom where a half-wall defined a kitchen area with play stove, sink, refrigerator, table, and chairs. As the children watched, Gail opened up all of the cabinets. "They're empty!" several children shouted out. "Where's all the food?" Gabriel asked. "And the plates and dishes and pans?" questioned Maya. Mark responded, "Mrs. Holtz and I have noticed lately that sometimes the way many of you play in this area is not very productive. Remember all of the times that one of us had to come over and help children settle down? So we decided to present you with a challenge: if there are no foods or dishes here, what will you play when you come to the dramatic play area? We're going to let you figure that out. We'll help you if you need any special materials. But how we use this area will be up to you as long as we see that you are working together in a safe way." They took the group back to the meeting area and let them make choices for their starting play areas. Five children chose the dramatic play area. "This ought to be interesting," Gail said to Mark. "I'll stay nearby to facilitate," Mark replied.

The five children went over to the dramatic play area. Some sat in chairs while others leaned against the stove and cupboards. "What are we going to do?" Maya asked. "We could ask to get all the stuff back," Gabriel suggested. "No, let's do something different," Andre suggested. "Like what?" David asked. "I know. Let's make our own food!" Leah suggested. A long discussion ensued about what they needed to make their own food. "How about playdough? We could make cookies and cakes and pies and . . . hey, I know. Let's make a bakery!" Everyone embraced Maya's idea. David and Andre were sent with Mark to get playdough, rollers, and cookie cutters. "What will we bake them on?" Leah asked. "We need some pans." Gabriel went off to the block area and returned with some long, flat blocks. "These could be our pans," he said. The children began rolling and pounding the playdough, forming cookie shapes with the cutters and making larger circles as pies and cakes. "I need to decorate my cake. It's a birthday cake," David said. He ran off to the art area and returned with pipe cleaners, colored tissue paper, glitter sprinkles, and small sticks. As he passed Mark, he called out, "Is this okay, Mr. Mason?" "Sure is, David. I see lots of thinking and planning going on in that bakery," Mark replied. The children played bakery for multiple days. The groups of children changed during that time and new ideas developed.

As we have seen, teachers have an important role in supporting and sustaining children's engagement in high-level play. Teachers can go even further than the actions we've identified. If high-level play is sustained, children are using imaginative play strategies, and little teacher intervention is needed. So a wise teacher may leave well enough alone. However, if there is any question that the play could go further, teachers may want to consider using provocations.

The use of provocations in this context is not meant to be something negative, such as aggravating or irritating the children. Rather, it is used here in the same way it is used by the practitioners who engage in the Reggio Emilia approach: as a stimulation or prompt to encourage children to engage more deeply in their play. In the Reggio Emilia approach, a teacher is seen as a "provocateur, one who 'complicates' the child's already complex thinking process, expands the notion of operating within the child's zone of proximal development. Indeed, such a reconceptualization suggests that the teacher may actually participate in stretching the limits of such a 'zone' through the presentation of challenges that require more active engagement and social negotiations" (New 1998, 273). Gail and Mark are examples of teachers who provoke children's thinking in play situations with very positive and interesting results.

Effective provocations are out of the ordinary, grabbing children's attention and communicating that the status quo is not to be maintained. They result from a teacher's careful observation that such a radical step is necessary. As in the example above, teachers may decide to use provocation because they have tried other interventions and not found them successful in facilitating high-level play. They want to use the provocation "to initiate a virtual outpouring of ideas, images, questions, and emotions" (Nimmo 1998, 302) on the part of the children. A teacher also may use a provocation because of interests the children have expressed or topics that have intrigued them. When deciding on a provocation for play, teachers need to know the children in their classroom well so they don't overwhelm them. In introducing provocations, teachers must also be ready to be partners and collaborators with the children, helping them get the materials they need, working out the roles they will engage in, and developing the play even further.

For preschoolers and kindergartners, four types of general provocations can work effectively to stimulate their play involvement:

- planning field trips and inviting special visitors
- using books
- offering new materials (or taking away materials)
- considering groupings of children

When thinking of other provocations, teachers need to consider the age of the children with whom they work. For example, younger three-year-olds may respond better to less radical changes in play experiences than older kindergartners. Some provocations that are appropriate for specific age groups are identified later in the chapter. Let's look now at the ones that tend to work well with children from ages three to six.

Field Trips and Special Visitors

Field trips and special visitors help extend the children's knowledge so they can incorporate new ideas in their play. But just going on the field trip to learn about the post office or having the nurse visit to talk about the doctor's office is not enough. Teachers need to help children focus on the roles and actions that people take in different situations. On the field trip to the post office, a teacher can point out the tasks of selling stamps and weighing packages at the counter as well as the sorting and preparing of mail for home delivery. When the nurse comes to visit, teachers can act out the role of patient as the nurse tends to their needs, checking temperature, blood pressure, and weight. The nurse can describe the different roles nurses and doctors take when working with their patients.

Interesting books can help expand children's understanding of people's roles in a variety of situations as well. Nonfiction books about doctors and hospitals with photographs and simple explanations of the roles people play in medical settings, the materials they use, and the experiences children might have in these settings can enhance the resulting dramatic play. In addition, long-term, in-depth studies of topics can provoke new play ideas as well. Many teachers combine such studies with field trips and visitors, so children develop a better understanding of a topic. For example, through their investigations, field trips, and visitors, the children learn how a dairy farm operates and what the various workers do. Then, they can more fully replicate what they've learned when they play at milking cows and bottling the milk.

Use Books as Provocations

Some well-loved children's stories can be used to provoke children's thinking as they play. Such stories may help children be more cohesive in developing their own play scenarios so that they have a beginning, middle, and end. Acting out *Goldilocks and the Three Bears* or *The Billy Goats Gruff* gives structure and content to a dramatic play episode. Cathy Boldger, a kindergarten teacher in Wisconsin, has three chairs of different sizes in her classroom. Each is decorated with an appropriate bear's face: Papa Bear, Mama Bear, and Baby Bear. The children love to act out the story on a regular basis.

It's important that teachers encourage the children to retell the story in their own way—even though it may not be true to the original version. As we've seen, imagination and creativity are important in reaching higher levels of play. If story lines get slightly mixed up, the play may very well be richer in nature. Books like *The True Story of the Three Little Pigs* by Jon Scieszka can stimulate children to consider the very different viewpoint of the big bad wolf in this story.

Books can stimulate play in other areas of the classroom as well. When I taught kindergarten, I would read *Rosie's Walk* by Pat Hutchins, and the children would act out the story, making paths with blocks to map out a route through the classroom just like the path that Rosie followed.

Offer New Materials

Offering new materials is another way to scaffold children's play so that it grows more complex and engaging. Consider the following scenario:

Manipulatives Play

Peng, Malia, and Cameron were playing with colorful plastic manipulatives at a table. They had three baskets of different manipulatives in front of them—and were pulling the items out of the baskets and making piles of them on the table. Each child had a pile that kept growing larger and larger. "I've got the most!" Malia called out. "No, I do!" shouted Peng. Miss Brown was watching nearby. She went to her cupboard and got three egg cartons from her supplies, walked over to the table, set them down without saying a word, and walked away. Cameron quietly started placing red items in one of the spaces in his carton and blue ones in another. Malia said, "I can do that too," and began sorting her items by color. Peng looked at the other two children and said, "Hey, how about we line these up? Then, I'll put all the blue ones in mine. You can put all the red ones in, Cam. Malia, what color do you want to do?" "Green and yellow," Malia said. "No, you can only do one color, right Peng?" Cameron asked. "No, she could put the green ones in one side and the yellow ones on the other side," Peng replied. They all agreed that this was acceptable and proceeded to sort all of the small objects on the table in this manner for approximately twenty minutes. When they were finished, they sought out Miss Brown. "Look, teacher! Look what we did." They excitedly showed her their filled egg cartons. "Wow, tell me about this," she said. They proceeded to describe to her what they had done.

In this scenario, all the teacher did was provide a new material. The children could have seen the egg cartons as an interruption to their play. Miss Brown would have known because they would have ignored them. However, in this case, the children changed their play to incorporate them. They had no need for further adult interaction until they asked Miss Brown for acknowledgment of what they had done. Miss Brown was watching closely to see what the children would do with the egg cartons, ready to step back in and support the children, if necessary.

As discussed in chapter 3, rotating in new materials periodically can be a way to set up conditions for high-level play, spark new interest in an area, or suggest new ways to build or role play. Making an on-the-spot decision to offer additional new materials as Miss Brown did can assist children in complicating their play. Pat, another preschool teacher, had only one telephone in her dramatic play area and had noticed a lot of competition for it among the children. She asked parents and colleagues if they had any old phones they no longer needed and ended up with quite a collection. The phone play in her room became extensive with some children engaged in two-way conversations with each other, and others in individual conversations with imaginary friends and family members. Pat noticed that some children were even familiar with features such as call-waiting and voice mail.

Sometimes a teacher must demonstrate ways to use the new materials or guide the children further with suggestions and ideas as in the following example:

Library Play

Some of the three-year-olds in Dianna's group had been taking books off the bookshelf and stuffing them into carrying bags. "We're going to the library, sister," Leyonna shouted out. "Okay, I gotta get some more books," Chelsea replied. Ling also filled her bag with books, and then all three went over to the playhouse area, pulled up chairs, and looked at their books for a short while. Then they took the books back to the shelves, dumped them out, and put new ones in their bags. The three girls played this scenario over and over again that day.

The next day, Dianna got out a date stamp, ink pad, and some index cards and took them over to the girls. "Would you like to set up a library so that you could help people check out books just like in the real library?" she asked. The girls responded enthusiastically and helped Dianna pull over another small table near the bookshelves and place a chair there. "Let's think about what librarians do when people want to check out books. Do you remember?" Dianna asked. Ling said, "They have to tell you when to bring the books back." "That's right, Ling. I know at our library they use a computer now, but we can use a date stamp. I brought a stamp and pad for you and some cards to stamp and put in the books so your customers will know when to bring their books back." With Dianna's help, the girls negotiated who would be the librarian first and talked through the actions they would take. Dianna showed them how to change the date on the stamp, roll it on the ink pad, make an imprint on the card, and place the card in the book. The girls took turns being the librarian, and other children joined in as customers as well. Dianna had to get out more books to accommodate all of the interest in the library play.

Dianna followed up on the girls' interest in libraries. Teachers who have prop boxes at the ready (as discussed in chapter 3) are able to quickly pull out new materials to support children's play themes.

Teachers do not have to go to great expense to find materials to support a play theme. It is well recognized that a higher level of play involves use of objects as symbols for other objects. Called "symbolic function," children "are able to use objects, actions, words, and people to stand for something else. . . . Vygotsky thought that this symbolic use of objects, actions, words, and people prepared the way for children to learn literacies based on the use of symbols like reading, writing, and drawing" (Bodrova and Leong 2007, 124). Kindergartners or children with lots of play experience may do this more in their play than younger preschoolers or less-experienced players. If Pat had not found as many phones as she needed, she could have suggested that the children use wooden blocks or small boxes as phones. She also could have tried to engage the children in making phones for themselves. In the following scenario, Tyler announces, "We're going camping" to the other players in the dramatic play area. His teacher did not have a prop box for that particular theme so she helped the children gather materials together that would enhance their play.

Camping Dramatic Play

Tyler, Calvin, and Joseph were playing in the house corner. "I'm the cooker," Joseph shouted out as he pulled out a pot from the cupboard and placed it on the stove. Using a wooden spoon, he stirred inside the pot. "I'm making chili," he said. Tyler and Calvin were busy putting on hats and buttoning up vests. "Come on, guys," Joseph said. "You gotta eat your chili." He put some bowls on the table but his guests did not sit down. "We're going camping," Tyler announced. "Right, Calvin?" "Yeah, we're going camping," Calvin agreed. And the two stomped off around the classroom. Teacher Mariella noticed that the camping play seemed to only involve moving around the classroom. She also noticed that Joseph continued to try to get the boys back to eat the chili and engage in his "cooker" play. To Tyler and Calvin, she said, "Hey guys, how about if Joseph is cooking for you back at the campsite and we make a tent for you to sleep in over there?" The boys responded enthusiastically and helped Mariella place a blanket over the table and find pillows for sleeping. "Joseph, do you want to cook on a camp stove or over a fire?" she asked. "A fire!" he replied. "What can we use to make a fire at your campsite?" asked Mariella. The boys discussed among themselves and Mariella suggested they go looking around the classroom to see what they might find. They returned with a few long wooden blocks that they set up to represent their fire. Joseph stirred his pot over the fire and served his bowls of chili to the boys as they sat inside their tent. The play continued with going to sleep, waking up, more cooking, and going to sleep again. Throughout, Joseph was always the cooker.

Using things that are already in the classroom (such as the blanket, table, and blocks) and helping the children to have them represent something else (the tent and the fire) is a way to extend their abstract thinking and use of symbols. It engages them on a higher cognitive level that requires imagination and problem solving.

Consider Groupings of Children

Another strategy that can help teachers facilitate mature, productive play is to consider the groupings of children. High-level play for children is often a social experience. They engage in role plays that require cooperation in order to play out the scene. They must reach some sort of agreement on roles and actions that may involve negotiation and compromise. Often, a child takes the role of play leader and directs the actions of others. This child may be more experienced in play, have more developed language skills, or have a more assertive personality. Usually, the other children follow this child's directions. In fact, in some play scenarios when the play leader leaves the scenario, the play ends. The others in the group cannot sustain the play without the play leader.

Remember the Golden Ticket story from chapter 4? The teachers in that preschool program were proactive in grouping children for play periods. They did not do this every day. They valued the natural flow of social relationships in their classroom and allowed children to choose play partners and areas most of the time. Then they observed closely as children played so they could get a sense of who chose what area and who took more of a lead in the play activities. They also paid attention to which areas certain children avoided. Periodically, they organized play groups and assigned play areas. As they did so, they thought about the children who were most comfortable in a play area and those who did not go there as often. This formed the basis of their groupings—each grouping had a more experienced player to potentially lead the play with others who were not as experienced. And remember that these teachers also noticed changes in children's play immediately and over the long term.

Whether a teacher formalizes different groupings of children at playtimes or encourages more natural changes in play partners, the dynamics of the group will influence what happens in the play.

Play can also cross cultural and linguistic barriers: there is a "cultural universal of play as a means for entering into a shared social life with other children" (Genishi and Dyson 2009, 64). In preschools and kindergartens where multiple home languages are represented, teachers can use grouping strategies to facilitate play. Teachers can make sure each child has a language partner—another child or an adult who speaks the same home language—who will help the child engage more fully in building a block structure or creating a dramatic play scenario. There are also ways to create group experiences in which all children can participate. Consider the following story from a preschool classroom:

Birthday Party

Sarine, an English speaker, announced to her friends, Melissa and Tina, that they were going to have a birthday party. They often played together, with Sarine in the play leader role. All three girls spoke English. Tina was bilingual and Sarine spoke a little Spanish. Dominga, the assistant teacher, was nearby and commented in Spanish about the girls' plans. Then Sarine said to Dominga, "You be the birthday girl." Dominga sat down at the table in the play kitchen, and the girls adorned her with scarves and jewelry. Soon other children joined the party. Many of them spoke only Spanish. Play food items, pots and pans, dress-up clothes, and other items from around the classroom were piled on the table in front of Dominga as her presents. Finally, Dominga said, "No mas," and led the group in singing "Las Mañanitas," the birthday song in Mexico. Dominga thanked everyone in both English and Spanish for her beautiful gifts and party. Then the children spent time putting everything back in its place. (Genishi and Dyson 2009, 61–62)

No matter what their home language, these children shared knowledge of birthday party customs and traditions. "One was hardly aware that the children spoke different languages, as they clearly understood the language and accompanying actions of 'birthday.' Dominga, as teacher, was responsive to the child players' incorporation of her into their play. She used both Spanish and English to extend the play and build on what the children were doing" (Genishi and Dyson 2009, 62). Facilitating play requires teachers to be ever mindful of the individual characteristics of the children in their groups. They can help children be more inclusive, as in the example above, and more successful by pairing language partners or more-experienced and less-experienced players. Such groupings allow children with different social and cultural backgrounds, strengths and weaknesses, and personalities and capabilities to "form a communicatively complex, unofficial world" (141) in their play.

Provocations for Younger Preschoolers

For younger preschoolers, or for children with less play experience, a successful provocation may not be as radical as one for older children. Instead, it may involve adding to their repertoire of play themes. Younger preschoolers tend to play what they know. They take on familiar roles, such as mommy, daddy, sister, brother, baby, dog, cat, grocery store clerk, and doctor. In addition, they may need real materials to fully engage in their play. They look for a real telephone (rather than using a block as a symbol for a phone). Their play scenarios are simple. They need coaching in how to extend their actions beyond what they know about people's roles. "Just because a child has experience with a specific situation does not mean that he is paying attention to the roles being enacted before him. He may be focusing on the interesting objects rather than what people do and say. Therefore, the only thing he can do is to play with the objects rather than develop the rich play scenario" (Bodrova and Leong 2007, 147). In play with blocks and manipulatives, children's constructions do not change much over time—they may build towers and houses from blocks, or cars and buses with manipulatives. They build what is familiar to them or what they have been successful building before.

For younger preschoolers, teachers may provoke new play ideas by suggesting different dramatic play and construction themes. For example, by providing the actual materials to play restaurant, a teacher may see more role play of restaurant experiences. Providing menus from neighborhood restaurants, actual order pads (available at big box stores in bulk), tablecloths and napkins, a chef's hat and apron, a cash register, and money gives children many options to play out a scene that includes the chef, server, cashier, and diners. In addition, children may need the further provocation of the teacher discussing exactly what each of the people do in their restaurant role and even acting out those roles for the children at large-group time.

In construction play with blocks and manipulatives, teachers can provoke children's thinking and extend their play more fully as well. Block play will move beyond the building of towers and walls that is typical of younger players if small manipulatives, such as farm or zoo animals, are provided. Then teachers can begin discussions with children about where such animals live and what they need to be safe and cared for. Books about farms and zoos can be read at group time and added to the block area. Leaving the farm or zoo constructions up for multiple days encourages children to add details as they learn more about farms and zoos. At the sensory table, young preschoolers and less-experienced players may be provoked to develop new play ideas if the sand and water are changed out for other interesting materials with different textures and possibilities for use. Sometimes just the change in materials is provocation enough to engage new interest and encourage children in new exploration. Other times, a teacher's involvement is necessary to provoke children's interest, such as demonstrating how to pop the bubbles in bubble wrap with a toy hammer.

Lists of possibilities for provocations to enhance dramatic play, construction play with blocks and manipulatives, and sensory play are included in appendix A. The lists include suggestions for younger preschoolers and less-experienced players and for older preschoolers and kindergartners.

Provocations for Older Preschoolers and Kindergartners

As children gain in play experience, they are able to internalize more. In dramatic play, they use items as symbols for other items more frequently than younger children do. They identify more fully the rules that govern the roles they are playing because their life experiences are a little broader and their thinking is more flexible. "By kindergarten, children should be able to create pretend scenarios and roles with much less physical support and with less involvement on the part of the teacher. . . . They are not just dealing with physical objects but are manipulating them mentally, as when they pretend that a block is a cell phone" (Bodrova and Leong 2007, 149). Older preschoolers and kindergartners use this ability for symbolic representation in constructive play with blocks and manipulatives as well. Their block structures are often labeled as something other than a tower. They consider and include more details when building familiar structures. They also attempt to represent more objects in their constructions with manipulatives. Provocations for this age group can be more radical in order to introduce challenges that will stretch their thinking, problem solving, and creativity, and make use of their growing skills.

For example, a provocation in dramatic play for older preschoolers and kindergartners is to replace dress-up clothes with pieces of fabrics in different sizes and interesting textures. Then, encourage the children to use the fabrics for their costumes as they figure out roles in various scenarios. Children of this age may also be able to plan their dramatic play scenarios and incorporate ideas from stories and books. Documenting their scenarios through photos and recording their retelling of the story they acted out can also extend their experience.

In block play, children can be encouraged to do physics experiments by building ramps and rolling cars, balls, or cylindrical blocks down them; testing out different slants; and measuring how far the objects roll. They can play the roles of architect, builder, and inspector as they construct. Teachers can model what these jobs involve, bring in books about them, and invite visitors who work in these fields so the play has meaning for the children. Gail and Mark used another provocation to encourage the kindergartners in their class to get more creative in the block area. They placed a big, blue piece of fabric shaped like a pond on the floor of the block area and encouraged the children to consider ways of building on, in, or over water. The bridges and structures that the children built were extensive. They sought out books about bridges and tunnels and built boats out of Legos to float on the water. Gail and Mark were delighted with the imaginative problem solving that the children showed.

At the sensory table, older preschoolers and kindergartners can apply their ability to move away from actual objects, apply their understanding of roles, and sustain longer engagement as well. Their fine-motor skills are more developed, so the use of eyedroppers and turkey basters, for example, for transferring water to containers of various sizes will hold their interest. They can also play the roles of construction workers. Wearing hard hats and goggles, they can move sand with small construction vehicles and make buildings with small blocks. They also can conduct experiments, hypothesizing how long a block of ice will take to melt or predicting the results of various color combinations when mixing colored water at the sensory table. More possibilities for provocations for older preschoolers and kindergartners in dramatic, constructive, and sensory play are listed in appendix A.

Provocations and Emotions

As we saw with the kindergarten bakery story, provocations sometimes spark an emotional response. This can be their power—they raise uncertainties and new possibilities. In a keynote address at the 2009 NAEYC Professional Development Institute, John Medina talked about the importance of improvising for children's healthy brain development. Provocations force children to improvise. What happens when all of the foods and dishes are taken out of the play kitchen? What can you do with measuring tapes in the block area? What familiar stories can you combine as you plan dramatic play with other children? In a way, provocations are like play itself: they present children with the unexpected. And researchers are finding that "play encourages flexibility and creativity that may, in the future, be advantageous in unexpected situations or new environments" (Wenner 2009, 29). As teachers support children in play, they also plan for provocations that will encourage this flexibility and creativity. "The result is a fluid, generative, dynamic curriculum that emerges as the interests and concerns of children and adults develop together" (Hendrick 1997, 47).

Sometimes provocations can become highly charged emotionally and produce very interesting results as in the following story from my kindergarten classroom:

No Boys Today

Over several weeks, I noticed that at Center Time only boys were going to the large block area of my classroom. Occasionally, a girl would wander over and attempt to get involved in building, but she was always off to the side of the boys. Eventually, she would leave. The boys did not include her in their constructive play. And it seemed that the girls who were interested in block play could not quite figure out how to enter into the boys' constructive play. I was deeply concerned about this, because I knew there were benefits for all children in the acts of constructing and building. I tried to encourage girls to choose the block area and was not successful. I went over and played at the block area myself, inviting girls to join me. But again, their engagement there was short-lived and did not continue if I left the area. I finally decided a provocation was in order.

On a Thursday morning, as the children arrived at school, a couple of the boys noticed a large sign taped up over the block shelves. They stood and looked at it for a while, unable to decipher its meaning. Finally, they sought out Kim, one of the readers in the room. Kim's face lit up with a big smile as she read out loud, "No boys today." "What?" the boys shouted and came running to me. I calmed the boys down and said that we were going to discuss this further at our group meeting time.

By the time our meeting began, the boys in the room were visibly agitated and the girls were walking taller than ever. It was an interesting contrast to see. I began the meeting by explaining what I had noticed over the last few weeks and going through the steps that I had tried to engage girls and boys in block play. Finally, with heartfelt conviction, I told the children how important I thought that block play was for both boys and girls. "And that's why I decided that from now on, Thursdays will be days where only girls can play in the block area. You boys are welcome to play anywhere else in the room today." Peng, an avid block player, raised his hand and asked, "Can we make it 'No girls allowed in the house?'" We debated that for a while until I raised the question, "Have there been times when you boys felt like you couldn't play in the house area because the girls wouldn't let you?" None could say they had, and all agreed it wouldn't be fair then to exclude girls from that play. As choices were made and Center Time began, grumblings were still heard from the boys but several of the girls smiled, laughed, and took off delightedly to the block area.

We continued with this plan once a week and the boys came to anticipate the one day without blocks. More and more girls chose building and constructing on Thursdays and extensive structures were made cooperatively. Sometimes we even left them up overnight to be added on to by the block players the next day. For the first week, the block area was still dominated by boys. By the time two weeks had passed, girls started joining in block play with boys successfully on a more regular basis. After the third week, I called a group meeting and proposed that we no longer needed the exclusion on Thursdays and all were in agreement. The provocation worked!

Provocations can be a way, then, to not only facilitate children to move to higher levels of play, but also to help them understand more about themselves, the community of the classroom, and the greater world in which they live. In play, children express cultural influences and social factors, including beliefs, values, biases, and stereotypes. "Play prepares children for the culture in which they live and reflects that culture. However, as children interact with people from other groups as well as view television and movies portraying other cultures, they try to understand the ideas of other people; they try to make sense of them in the context of their own culture" (Bowman 2004, 130). Adults need to help children with this process and provocations such as the one above can be a way of doing so. Here's an example of the awareness of a four-year-old to the differences he sees in the people around him:

A Conversation

While washing hands and using the bathroom, Jaden said to his teacher, "Everyone in our class is white, except for me." The teacher responded, "Not everyone is white; we are all different. Keshuan is American Indian, Ms. Yolanda is Hispanic, and Jackson is African American just like you." He said, "But my skin is darker than Jackson's." "Yes it is. Everyone's skin color is a little different; that is what makes us unique." He thought for a minute and said, "My mom is Hispanic, like Ms. Yolanda."

The teacher talked openly and respectfully about the differences Jaden noticed, welcoming his thoughts and supporting his thinking. The book *Anti-Bias Education for Young Children and Ourselves,* by Louise Derman-Sparks and Julie Olsen Edwards (2010), gives many ideas for addressing issues around culture, bias, and stereotypes. It's important to provide materials that reflect the cultural backgrounds of the children in the classroom, to invite families to share their experiences and heritage, and to explore the world beyond so that children have a window on the lives of families different from their own. In addition, challenging exclusionary behaviors and valuing all children in a caring classroom community are essential tasks for teachers. "Teachers who use an antibias approach to curriculum recognize the importance of celebrating cultural differences, and they also believe that it's essential to help young children understand and confront the social and cultural biases facing them" (Pelo and Davidson 2000, 1–2).

When observing play, teachers may need to confront assumptions, such as "Girls can't do that" or "Daddies don't do that." They may find they need to mediate in disagreements about fairness. The egocentricity of young children requires a caring and observant adult who can help them negotiate the waters of disagreement and begin to see others' perspectives. Teachers may need to offer friendly reminders, or they may need to go much further and provoke the children's thinking. For example, a teacher might decide to add a wheelchair to the dramatic play area when children are pretending their legs don't work, or to bring in photographs of female professional athletes when children are focused only on male athletes (Pelo and Davidson 2000). In play, children reflect what they have experienced and, unfortunately, bias, stereotype, and injustice are all part of the human experience. Teachers in preschools and kindergartens cannot sit quietly by as scenarios with these issues play out.

The Power of Emotions and Play

Young children have many feelings and do not always know how best to express them. So, in their play they act them out: "drama comes to the door of every school with the child" (Singer and Lythcott 2004, 80). Play can be beneficial to children's emotional development. The enjoyment children experience in play relieves stress and anxiety. And when pretending, frightening feelings can be dealt with in safe ways. Preschool and kindergarten teachers often see children's feelings expressed in play situations. The scripts that are developed in family play often reflect moments in the child's home where heated exchanges occurred between parents, or worries were expressed. In constructive play, children who know about or have experienced such events as terrorist attacks, earthquakes, tornadoes, or floods build and destroy their block structures again and again. Consider the following excerpt:

> Because the children have not learned to distinguish between feelings
> and concepts, they cannot adequately separate themselves as thinkers
> from their thoughts about the world. The reason imaginative play is so
> appealing to preschool children is that their feelings and ideas can coexist
> in harmonious confusion. Fears or unfulfilled wishes can be projected

into a familiar reality and, at the same time, new ideas about reality can be explored within a context of emotional security. Pretend play is used to replay events, replay bad experiences, cope with anger and jealousy, and gain real power. (Segal 2004, 45)

High-level play can help children cope with events and situations that feel out of their control. The self-regulation required by cooperative dramatic play or extensive constructive play keeps feelings and impulses in check. In order to continue acting within the evolving script with other children, a child must function within her role so that the play can continue to be successful. If she loses such control, she may lose her play partners. And most preschoolers and kindergartners are motivated to keep an enjoyable play situation going. If a child cannot self-regulate, then the play often becomes chaotic and out of control; an adult needs to provide safety and stability so the child can calm herself and rejoin the play situation. She also may need adult help to re-enter the play with her peers.

It's important that teachers recognize the importance of emotions in play and pay attention to the ways children express their feelings. Facilitating play experiences may feel like a therapy session at times. Using reflective statements, such as "Boy, that teddy bear sure is angry," and asking questions to get more information, such as "What's he so angry about?" will help the child much more than intervening with limits and rules (for example: "We don't pound our teddy bears like that." And, "Remember to use your inside voice"). Providing safe places to express feelings and appropriate materials to do so is also helpful. Puppets, dolls, and stuffed animals can help children act out intense feelings. The adult may need to model for the child how to use them before the child is able to do so. A pounding pillow can be provided for expressing frustrations. A quiet, safe place can be set up for moments when playing with others feels overwhelming. Talking and singing about feelings in large- and small-group times can help children develop the vocabulary words for emotions. And encouraging children to draw and paint what they are feeling can provide other outlets.

When a teacher knows that a child has experienced a traumatic event, using play experiences may help the child process the intense feelings that result. My own son was in a school bus accident at six years of age. His favorite toy became a turtle puppet whose head could go in and out of its shell. My son's counselor used this soft puppet extensively to encourage my son to talk about his fears and worries about safety. And when those fears and worries became too much, the turtle would retreat into the safety of its shell. For many weeks, the turtle puppet was a constant companion. Here's an example of teachers in a preschool program responding with a play experience for a young three-year-old who had experienced an upsetting event:

The Elevator Story

Jeremy's mother called ahead to the preschool and spoke with Jeremy's teachers before school that day. She reported that in their high-rise building, Jeremy ran ahead and got on the elevator as she locked the door to their apartment. By the time she reached it, the elevator doors had closed and it had gone down to the lobby with Jeremy in it. Being just three, Jeremy was very frightened. Luckily, the doorman, a familiar figure, was in the lobby and kept Jeremy with him until his mom came down. However, Jeremy had a rough night, clinging to his mother, not sleeping well, and expressing worries that this might happen again.

Jeremy's teacher, Marie, got out the play garage (which has an elevator) from the block area and some people figures (a mother, a child, and a man). When Jeremy came to school, she greeted him warmly and encouraged his mother to stay as long as he needed her to. And she addressed the situation right away. "It sounds like you had a scary thing happen yesterday in your elevator. I bet that worried you when those doors closed. Did you miss your mom?" Jeremy nodded his head. "But your doorman, Tom, was waiting for you downstairs, wasn't he?" Again, Jeremy nodded. Marie took him over to the play garage. "See, in our garage we have an elevator just like in your building. And look, here's Tom waiting at the bottom just for you. Do you want to put the little boy in the elevator and make him go up and down? The mommy's at the top and Tom's at the bottom." Jeremy became quite engrossed in making the elevator go up and down. At first, the boy figure went alone. Then the mother joined him. The tension on Jeremy's face began to relax as he played. "Can Mom go now so you can play at school?" Marie asked. Jeremy gave his mother a hug and ran off to join another group of friends at the water table.

Play helps children feel more powerful. In this example, Jeremy was in control of the elevator as he played, unlike in the real-life experience. He regained confidence as he controlled whether the boy figure was alone or with the mother. Children often choose to act out powerful roles too. Moms, dads, and teachers are often portrayed as mean and demanding. Children feel powerful in bossing "the children" (themselves) around in play. Everyday heroes, such as firefighters, police officers, doctors, and nurses, are engaging because they take care of children in frightening situations. But perhaps most appealing are superheroes like Batman, Spiderman, or Power Rangers. The marketing of TV shows and movies very cleverly appeals to young children's desire to be powerful. Superhero play or any kind of powerful figure play can reach the higher levels of productive play—but it also can be out of control or simplistic and imitative.

From my own teaching experience (back in the days of Teenage Mutant Ninja Turtles), I know that the constant imitation of fighting the bad guys and replaying the latest TV show can be frustrating for teachers. Yet I've also seen how this play can be made more complex by thoughtful teacher interventions. Here is a description of some of my experiences as I coped with children's Ninja Turtle play in my kindergarten classroom. I think the strategies work with even the latest, most popular superheroes.

Coping with Ninja Turtle Play

Much of my time as a kindergarten teacher was spent facilitating problem solving among my children around their aggressive play. This play seemed to begin innocently enough, either as superheroes acting out or as war play, but it deteriorated quickly into outright aggression and injury.

The children's play did not appear to be imaginative, rich, or inventive. Rather, I saw imitations of cartoon characters, TV shows, and horror movies. I was also concerned about the stereotypical male/female roles in the daily chase games on our playground.

My interventions followed what I considered to be good early childhood practice. I emphasized a pacifist viewpoint: "Weapons hurt people, and I don't want any of my friends to get hurt, even in pretend play. Use your words to solve problems, or get a teacher if you need help." The children would nod their heads, mimic my words back to me, and then go off and play the same games, but more surreptitiously, so I wouldn't see.

I explained to the children in my class that I wanted to understand more about why children like to play Teenage Mutant Ninja Turtles and chase games and that I wanted to interview them. I had thirty volunteers the first day! During class developmental writing time, I wrote in my journal about my decision to watch the cartoon show every day, and I drew a very poor representation of one of the characters. I was immediately surrounded by the "Turtle experts"—the children fervently informing me of many specifics. I responded with curiosity and openness to the many "lessons" the children gave me. The children's active play seemed to change almost immediately after I shared my interest.

The aggressiveness of the play lessened. I was able to introduce the concept of stuntmen and stuntwomen who practice very carefully planned fake fights. I engaged the children again using the lingo of their play. The class aide and I were able to engage children in conversations that allowed us to explore the children's perception about superheroes. We expressed acceptance of their thoughts, but we also asked questions that encouraged them to be critical viewers: Why do the Turtles have to use weapons and fight so much? and Are there other ways they could solve their problems with Shredder? I felt more comfortable including Turtle words in our writing. I used these word lists as a way to encourage the children to move beyond the TV scripts and stereotypical superhero behaviors they were exhibiting. Children began to write stories that took on the rich, imaginative aspect that I felt had been missing in their play. Their dramatic play was influenced by what they had written, and they began to combine more characters from the various stories.

Superhero play can be bewildering and frustrating to teachers. We see its necessity for children as a way for them to feel powerful in a scary world, yet we also try to maintain a safe, caring environment. I could educate parents about my concerns and lobby the networks and producers of the TV shows and movies. However, I could not leave the young children with whom I worked without a caring adult to help them construct their own understanding of violence and aggression.

I advocate that teachers take a variety of actions regarding superhero play in their classrooms. Our acceptance of their interests will give our voices far greater power and meaning to them when we discuss alternative ways to approach the aggression and violence shown in the media. Teachers can encourage parents to buy open-ended toys that lead to rich, creative play for children, rather than buy television-related toys that limit children's ideas to the scripts of the shows. (Gronlund 1992, 21–25)

In his book, *Magic Capes, Amazing Powers*, Eric Hoffman (2004) offers many suggestions for working with superhero play so that it becomes safer and much more imaginative and complex.

To get children started on dramatic play that has more of a fantasy component, treasure hunting is always a great way to begin. Gold- and silver-painted rocks, wood, and walnuts; large, colored beads; fake jewels; or shells can be buried in a sensory table or sandbox, tied into bushes, or hidden under furniture. Children can also hide them from adults. Older children enjoy making treasure maps and cardboard treasure boxes. The children can dig, sift, or use magnets, nets, or tongs to capture the treasure. Treasure hunting works well with a variety of dramatic play themes—pirates, castles, elves and fairies, and even field mice. (92)

Hoffman also uses a provocation to help children move beyond the use of guns and weapons in their superhero play by providing them "with props and play opportunities that expand their idea of what is powerful" (102). He suggests that teachers and children work together to create items that give the players strength and power. For example

- Make "power bracelets" of stretchable trim fabrics, beads, and shells, or buy lots of cheap plastic and metal bracelets.
- Provide a variety of scarves (with Velcro added to the corners) to be made into capes, skirts, headbands, and belts.
- Decorate hats, headbands, and paper crowns with jewels, glitter glue, and feathers.
- Make wands from rolled-up colored papers, twisted pipe cleaners, or pieces of foam.
- Create badges and medals out of juice can or jar lids, thick cardboard, or large poker chips. Spray paint them silver or gold and tie them on ribbons, yarn, or strips of decorative cloth.
- Make magic buttons by gluing a button or bottle cap to a small, decorated piece of wood or cardboard.

- Have a collection of magic objects such as painted or polished rocks and twigs, old keys, coins, decorated thread spools, and old watches. (Hoffman 2004, 102–3)

The materials themselves will not change the play—but a teacher who helps children create stories using such materials will have far more impact on leading the children to go beyond the imitation of the latest TV cartoon show or hit movie. These materials welcome the underlying theme of superhero play—one of children exploring what it means to be powerful in a frightening world. And the materials fuel their imaginations to create their own characters and stories and move to high-level, complex play.

Teachers can lead children to engage in even higher-level play by provoking their thinking with new ideas and by building on the emotional power of play experiences. The next chapter looks at the ways that adding representation through documenting, writing, and drawing can further enrich children's play.

CHAPTER 7

Adding Representation to Further Enrich Play

> Teachers must remain alert to the child's ever expanding reach, and stay one step ahead. (New 1998, 273)

Terri has added writing materials to all of the play areas of her preschool classroom. She encourages the children to use them in ways that complement their play. If they are acting out doctors and nurses, she suggests that they write prescriptions and orders for special tests. If they are building with manipulatives, she asks if they would like to draw what they built when they are finished so they can have a record of it to post on a bulletin board or to take home and show to their parents. Sometimes she takes a photograph and asks the child to describe the construction, thus serving as a scribe who takes dictation from the child and shows him or her how the spoken word can be written down. Terri is certain that by adding these materials and making these suggestions, the play in her classroom has reached a higher level.

Most of the children in Marilyn's kindergarten are interested in writing and drawing. She starts each day with journal writing and encourages children to draw and write about their play. If she sees them create an interesting scenario building pirate ships and acting out a hunt for a treasure chest, she makes some notes about what she saw and shares them with the children. She can see that her documentation validates what the children were playing and models the writing process for them. They ask her how to spell certain words to incorporate in their own writing and have even begun to do such writing in their play. She lets them keep their pirate ship construction up over several days. As the play deepens, she notices that the children add writing and drawing to their activities, making treasure maps and signs as well as pirate flags.

Representation—documenting on paper through writing, drawing, or photography—takes children's play experiences further along the spectrum of high-level play. Some of the provocations identified in the last chapter involved representation, such as asking children to draw their block structures or their creations with manipulatives. Teachers can add representation to the play process by documenting dramatic play scenarios with photos and children's comments. Remember the Kindergarten Bakery story from the previous chapter? The play had continued for over a week when the teachers decided to add representation to the experience. Here's what happened:

Kindergarten Bakery, continued

As children created cookies, pies, and cakes with playdough, Gail and Mark encouraged them to let their baked goods dry and harden and then sell them to each other. Play money was exchanged between the customers and bakers. The play continued to be productive, with many children engaged in production and sales at the bakery. At their Friday planning meeting, Gail and Mark decided to take the already successful play in this area to an even higher level and add written representation to this process.

At meeting time the following Monday morning, Gail announced, "Before we make our choices for centers today, Mr. Mason and I have an announcement. We have changed something in the dramatic play area again." The children groaned.

"Not again," Andre said. "We like our bakery." "Oh, we haven't changed the bakery," Mark replied. "We've just added something new—order forms and delivery boxes. If you're interested in joining us to find out more, please choose the bakery for your center." And several children enthusiastically did.

Bakery Order Form

CAKES

Cake Flavor	Frosting Color
☐ chocolate	☐ blue
☐ vanilla	☐ green
☐ strawberry	☐ pink
	☐ yellow

Needed on: Monday Tuesday Wednesday Thursday Friday

Name _____

Bakery Order Form

PIES

☐ apple	☐ blueberry
☐ cherry	☐ lemon

Needed on: Monday Tuesday Wednesday Thursday Friday

Name _____

At the bakery center, Gail introduced the four forms she had produced: one for cookies, pies, cakes, and muffins. As she showed them to the children, a discussion ensued on how people might place their orders. "They could put an X next to what they want," Maya suggested. "Yes, they could. But how would you know how many cakes or pies they might want?" asked Gail. "You have to write the number or make that many lines," Andre said. The group agreed. In addition, the days of the week were listed across the bottom of the form. "Be sure you circle the day when you will have their order ready and delivered," Gail reminded them.

The children took great interest in going around the classroom with their order forms and collecting orders. Sometimes they wrote a child's name on the form; sometimes the child wrote his or her own name. Then the bakers returned to the bakery center to fill the orders. Gail and Mark had scrounged up several cardboard boxes to use for deliveries. Sometimes the children were able to fill the orders with the already hardened creations; other times they needed to make new ones out of fresh playdough. As before, many other materials were used to decorate the baked goods. Dark paper punches were used for chocolate chips on the cookies. Yellow tissue paper was crunched up as lemon filling for the lemon meringue pies. As the orders were filled, they were delivered to children around the classroom. Everyone played along, pretending to eat their goodies and sharing them with their friends (and then returning them to the bakery for further use). The order forms added a level of engagement, structure, and representation that had not been there in the play before and extended the children's interest for another week.

Bakery Order Form

MUFFINS

☐ banana ☐ cinnamon

☐ blueberry ☐ strawberry

Needed on: Monday Tuesday Wednesday Thursday Friday

Name _____

Bakery Order Form

COOKIES

☐ chocolate chip ☐ oatmeal

☐ gingerbread ☐ sugar

Needed on: Monday Tuesday Wednesday Thursday Friday

Name _____

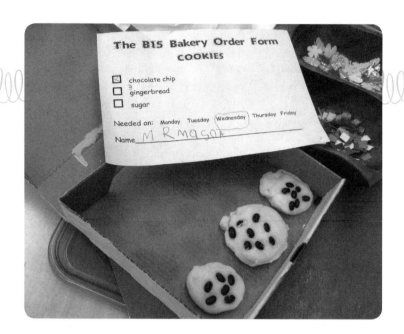

Gail and Mark complicated the bakery play in a way that was just right for the kindergarten children. They knew the children's abilities with writing and mathematical representation and gave the children a meaningful experience for representation in their dramatic play.

What does representation add to play experiences? It adds validity and importance to what children are doing. It adds an intellectual dimension and level of challenge requiring a child to consider, "How will I communicate this to others so that they know what I was thinking, doing, imagining as I acted out this role or built this structure?" And it communicates that this is something to be recorded and remembered. Vygotsky and his followers encourage the use of drawing and writing "to help children structure and clarify new ideas" (Bodrova and Leong 2007, 72). Mathematical representation can also be a part of enriching children's play. Numerals as written symbols represent specific quantities. Geometric shapes and mathematical problems can be represented in a variety of ways. Playing with both written language and mathematical symbols provides children with opportunities to learn and explore academic concepts in a playful way.

Here are some ways teachers can add representation to the play process:

- Use photos of children's play in action to enrich the play and to create documentation displays.
- Add writing and drawing materials to play experiences.
- Write for children through scripts and anecdotes.
- Create a climate of acceptance for children's representational skills and scaffold their writing efforts.
- Encourage mathematical representation with materials as well as with numerals and mathematical symbols.

The elements that representation can add are important and exciting. When a teacher suggests representation to children at play, she may find that she turns what may have been simplistic play into something much richer. Chapter 2 included the story of Leyonna and Amber's repetitive play in the housekeeping area. In that situation, the teacher, Della, suggested that the girls make grocery lists and the girls suggested items for Della to write.

Even when the adult writes down words dictated by children, the play becomes richer. The official nature of such documentation gives it importance and requires children to think about what they are saying in the context of the play. This is more cognitive engagement on the part of the children. Leyonna and Amber were going grocery shopping and thus had to sort and categorize in their own minds, based on their own experiences, what can be purchased at a grocery store. They didn't suggest baseballs, Frisbees, and swim fins. They suggested food items and household goods instead. And in the process of this thinking, they became more invested in the play scenario taking it to the higher levels of play that Della was striving for.

A note of caution needs to be given, however, about representation. Teachers need to take care not to change a play experience into an academic lesson led by the teachers. The play content should still be mostly determined and enacted by the children. The representation should go along with the play content as in the bakery story, or add more depth to what the children are doing as in the grocery shopping story. If Leyonna and Amber had not responded positively to Della's suggestion of grocery shopping and making lists, Della would not have forced the issue. She would have stepped back and considered another way to help the girls move beyond their repetitive actions and simplistic serving play. Writing and drawing should enhance and sustain the play—not interrupt it—just as all of the other interventions suggested in this book are meant to do.

Photos and Documentation Displays

Taking a photograph of what a child is doing is another way of validating his actions and encouraging him to continue. In fact, teachers who document through photography often find that children will call out as they play, "Take my picture. Over here!" Teachers may have to gently remind children that they cannot take photos of everyone all the time. Photographs are a form of representation that captures ethereal moments in play. Usually, constructions made with blocks or manipulatives are taken apart at cleanup time. Photographs of these moments in play keep them alive so they can be revisited again and again. Photos of children in dramatic play scenarios with their descriptions of what was occurring can be another way for them to preserve memories and maybe even build on the play another day.

Here's an example of the power of photography in children's play:

Test Crash

Several three- and four-year-old children are seated at a table building with Duplos. Robbie and Bryce announce that they are making jet fighters and crash their constructions into one another, destroying them, and laughing. They then grab the pieces and build their "fighters" again. Teacher Racquel sits down and says, "Hey, tell me what's going on over here. What are you building?" Janie says, "I'm building a house." Racquel asks, "Where's the door? Oh, there it is. Who lives in your house, Janie?" As she and Janie talk, Robbie and Bryce crash their fighters again. Racquel says, "Boy, your fighters keep breaking apart when they crash. I wonder if there's a way to build them so that they are stronger. Did you know that the men and women who build airplanes have to work very hard to make their planes so that they are safe? How could you make your planes so that they are safe?" Racquel helps the boys choose parts and then test the connections and sturdiness without crashing. She explains that it's too expensive to do a crash test every time. The engineers have to do other kinds of tests. She then suggests that they take photographs of their different designs so they can remember them and display them for others to see. All of the children at the table start building constructions and asking her to photograph them. They become much more interested in this aspect of the play and the crashing stops. (Gronlund and James 2008, 56)

In this case, photography helped the children to settle down in their play and become more purposeful. Teachers can use photos to create documentation displays, adding children's drawings or work samples along with explanations and children's dictation. In the Reggio Emilia and Project Approaches, such documentation is an important aspect of teaching and learning. In the Project Approach, documentation displays are identified to serve three functions:

1. to provide information that children can refer to in their work and play
2. to reflect children's growing experience of the project and show a developing record or diary of the work

Documenting Children's Learning
Exploring with Color and Paint

In Prekindergarten, we like to begin the school year by exposing the children to a variety of materials. We began with an exploration of paint by introducing the children to a variety of paint tools. As our first introduction to painting and color, we gathered on the tan rug where the colors red, blue, and yellow were carefully mixed in baby food jars to create new colors.

During our first painting day, we introduced *cool colors* to paint our large mural. With a large piece of paper spread out on the table, we used *big brushes* to paint the cool colors onto the paper.

The next day, after the mural had a chance to dry, We used *warm colors* and *small brushes*, to layer the warm colors over the cool colors on the mural.

The children enjoyed experimenting with the varied sized brushes, creating different sized lines.

3. to communicate the children's discoveries and achievements to particular audiences (their own teacher and classmates, other teachers and classes, the principal or head teacher, parents, or any other visitors to the school) (Katz and Chard 1997, 117)

Documentation of children's play experiences can have the same communicative power as that focused on a particular study topic or investigation. Not only does it communicate the value of play experiences to the children, but also to parents, community members, and school and program administrators. Chapter 8 looks at how to incorporate early learning standards and curricular goals into such displays as well.

Writing for Children through Scripts, Anecdotes, and Dictation

In many cases, teachers need to do writing or drawing for children as they play, bringing representation to the experience to enrich what the children are doing. Chapter 1 described how Doug scripted the children's camping play. Doug sat nearby and wrote down what the children said and did as they acted out a camping experience. Doug did not take shorthand—he just tried to get down the gist of the children's scenario as best he could. Then at group time, he announced, "I have a special story to read to everyone today," and read, "Once upon a time, there were three children who wanted to go camping. Their names were Lucia, Marco, and Robert." "Hey, that's me!" Marco called out and sat up tall, smiling. Doug continued with an account of the camping trip. The delight of the three children involved spread to all of the other children as well. Doug was validating the camping play and communicating its importance by not only recording it, but also by sharing it with the class. Other children began to call out to Doug during playtimes, asking if he would write down what they were doing. Doug accommodated when he could—when he wasn't needed to facilitate other play areas. He also saved the scripts in a three-ring binder and placed it in the library. Later, he added photographs as well. In his classroom, that binder became a favorite book to read.

Vivian Gussin Paley scripted much of her kindergarten children's play and studied it in depth, trying to understand the themes that the children wove through their dramas. She not only read the scripts back to the children, but also encouraged them to act them out. This gives another sense of importance and value to the children's dramatic play and helps them develop more of a sense of story. "Storytelling is easy to promote when there is a tangible connection to play" (1984, 2).

Preschool and kindergarten teachers are careful observers. They know that to assess children's capabilities and progress they need to watch them as they engage in a variety of activities. And they know that memory sometimes gets cloudy, so many times they write down brief notes or anecdotes about what they see children do or hear them say. The very act of writing anecdotes in front of children communicates the importance of their play. In fact, when children ask teachers what they are writing, teachers can answer with something like: "What you are doing is so interesting to me that I don't want to forget about it. So, I'm writing it down."

Reading the anecdotes to children is another way of making literacy connections for them. It shows that their play has value and gives them encouragement to continue what they are doing. Anecdotes can then be added to accompany the photographs of what children were doing and the drawings of their constructions. All of this can become part of a child's assessment portfolio, scrapbook, or ongoing file, which can be shared with family members in conferences or at the end of the school year.

Sometimes when teachers share anecdotes, children suggest things that the teacher should write down. They give dictation. The same can happen when children don't feel confident about writing something for themselves—the teacher becomes the scribe and writes word for word what the child says. Again, the connection between oral and written language is made, and children see the permanence of their words. In addition, they witness the teacher modeling the many conventions of print, including the formation of letters, spaces between words, and the use of capitalization and punctuation.

If a teacher talks through the process of writing, these literacy connections are reinforced even more. For example, as the child dictates, the teacher might say, "Oh, it sounds like you are asking a question so I'll have to put a question mark at the end of that sentence. Do you see that? That's a question mark. Okay, now what did you say next? Oh, I have to start the new sentence with a capital letter and when I write Alicia's name, it will start with a capital A, won't it?" When teachers share this mental processing with the children, they invite them to consider more of the writing process as their words are documented on paper.

Add Writing and Drawing Materials to Play Experiences

Teachers can encourage children to do their own representation as they play by adding writing materials to the play areas of the classroom. Young children play with representation through drawing and writing, figuring out how to best use their fine-motor skills in manipulating different types of drawing and writing tools to express themselves on paper. They experiment with the symbols of their written language and imitate the writing styles and purposes of adults. "In learning to write, children have to deliberately reflect on and consciously choose signs that will help them represent and communicate their intentions. Young children more readily experience the deliberate manipulation of symbolic stuff in dramatic play and, then, in drawing, block building, and other means of constructing symbolic worlds. These experiences can support and augment their efforts to use, and to differentiate, the particular strengths of writing" (Genishi and Dyson 2009, 83–84).

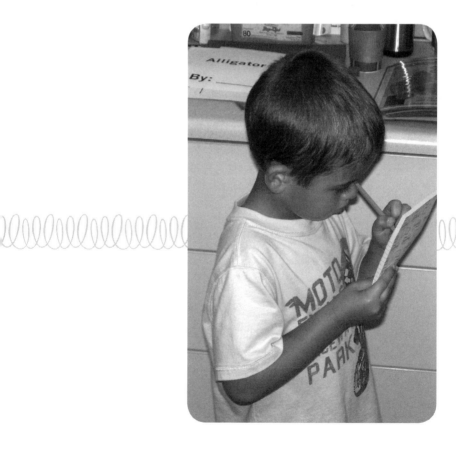

Younger preschoolers often see drawing as writing. "Look, I wrote a tree," a three-year-old says as he points to a drawing of a stick with a circle on the top. He represented a thought on paper—his definition of writing. As they get to be four and five, children begin to distinguish between the two processes but still may incorporate them together. So, for our purposes here, we will assume that children both write and draw together. Teachers' efforts to support children's representations are much the same whether the children are drawing, writing, or doing both.

Providing different kinds of paper and writing tools in play areas may bring about writing behaviors. "Well-crafted and print-enriched play centers that incorporate literacy roles, objects, and routines provide opportunities for children to explore and practice the functions and features of written language" (Kagan and Lowenstein 2004, 69). To create a well-crafted and print-enriched play center, teachers need to think in terms of the kind of writing that makes sense for the activities in each play area, rather than just putting paper and pencils or markers in centers. If the dramatic play area is set up as a family home, the writing materials should match that focus. If it is a doctor's office, those materials should change accordingly. Here's a list of possible writing materials for a family home area:

- a variety of writing tools, including pencils, pens, and markers
- stationery, cards, and envelopes for letter writing
- scrap paper and tablets for making grocery lists and taking telephone messages
- index cards for writing recipes
- checkbooks for paying bills
- calendars for keeping track of appointments

The placement of these materials is important too. A tablet and pen near the play phone communicate the possibility of message taking. Index cards and cookbooks in the kitchen cupboards give children the idea that they can write down recipes. Designating a desk area to house the writing tools, stationery, stamps, calendar, and checkbook encourages children to imitate letter writing and bill paying. And tablets placed near grocery circulars may entice children to make grocery lists. Appendix B gives many ideas for writing materials to accompany various dramatic play themes.

Writing materials can be added to the block area as well. Children can draw plans for their constructions before they are built, imitating architects and building planners. Or they can draw their constructions after the fact. In addition, buildings have addresses, and most have names. Providing paper, markers, and tape for sign making invites children to give addresses and names to their buildings and to sign their own names as the architects. When they build familiar structures and label them as a fast-food restaurant or pizza place, they can make a sign with the name for all to see. Signs can also be used to save buildings overnight. In more than one of the classrooms in which I taught, custodians often found block structures with signs the children made asking them to leave the buildings undisturbed and to clean around them. We even did this when we had double sessions each day. The morning class would leave a sign up for the afternoon class, telling them about the structure and inviting them to add on or change it in the afternoon. Many fun surprises evolved as each group added new ideas to the others' constructions.

Some teachers have a specially designated place such as a shelf or tray that they label "The Saving Place" or "Work in Progress." When children make something out of Legos or other connecting materials, they can label it with their name and a description, and place it on the saving tray or shelf until the next day.

When children create patterns and shapes out of colored blocks or beads, they can draw those shapes on paper to display or take home. In some classrooms, teachers ask children to draw or write to tell others what they did with that particular set of manipulatives. In a class of three-year-olds I worked with for several weeks, Evan drew pictures representing his work with a marble run. Here's his story along with his drawings:

Evan and the Marble Run

Once a week, we brought out a set of plastic connecting ramps and tubes in this class for three-year-olds. We teachers knew it took some experience with these materials before children were able to figure out how best to set up the foundational towers needed for the marbles to flow down the ramps successfully. We decided to devote one adult, me, to help children play in this area to increase the chances of success and avoid frustrations. Evan was one of the first to choose to play at the marble run every week that it was available.

I set up the first towers and demonstrated how to best make the marble roll downward. I encouraged Evan and the other children to connect pieces together and helped them problem solve when the marble got stuck or rolled off the end of a tube not connected to others. At the end of the first day of play, I asked Evan if he would like to draw or write about what he did with the marble run. He agreed and drew the first picture, saying the large orange dot was the marble.

As weeks went by, Evan learned to set up the towers by himself and created complex marble runs with marbles rolling back and forth, through whirligigs and loop-de-loops all the way to the bottom. He smiled and clapped, jumping up and down as the marble followed the path he had designed. After four weeks of working with these materials, I asked him if he wanted to draw or write about what he had done. He agreed and drew the second picture—but as he began to hand it to me, he stopped and said, "No, not this one. This is a bad one." He turned the paper over and drew the third picture and described it to me. "The marble starts here," he said, pointing to the right corner of his drawing. "There's tracks," he added as he traced down to the lower left corner where he ended saying, "And the marble stops here." He also pointed to symbols in the upper left corner saying, "Here's my name."

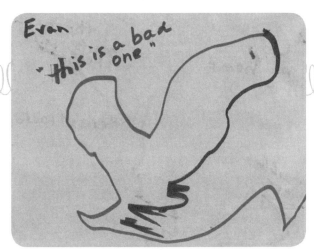

Evan
"this is a bad one"

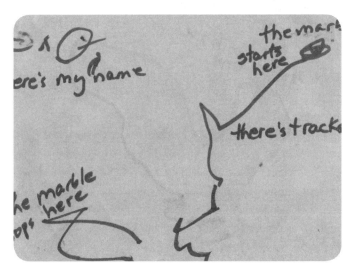

ere's my name

the mark
starts
here

there's track

he marble
ops here

Evan represented on paper what he had learned from his experiences building marble runs—the tubes and pieces had to create a downward path for the marble to roll successfully. The drawing made his understanding visible and clear to others.

Writing/drawing materials can be added to the sensory table as well to encourage children to record findings as they experiment with mixing water with sand or adding colors to shaving cream. More formal explorations (such as to see what sinks and floats) can be set up with recording sheets for representing the findings. Science journals—a place where children can record findings as they work at the sensory table—can be a part of children's everyday experiences that adds representation to the play process.

Create a Climate of Acceptance and Scaffold Children's Writing Efforts

In some classrooms, writing materials are placed throughout the classroom and yet the children do not use them. This may be because the adults have not set up the climate so that children's efforts at writing are accepted, or becuase the adults have not scaffolded children's efforts at written representation. For preschoolers and kindergartners, an adult's help is needed to make representation worthwhile. Children's emerging writing skills and experiments with representational drawing need much scaffolding from teachers. Without such support, children may give up in frustration and failure when their attempts do not look the same as the writing and drawing of adults. These two factors—setting the climate and scaffolding—are essential in bringing about more use of writing in children's play.

> Literacy, like other learning, is embedded in social relationships. When adults and children focus together on literacy activities using complex ideas and language, children's interest is high and their learning is increased. . . . Children who are most likely to learn to read easily and well have caregivers who are literate and can model the use of print; who endow print activities with both emotional and social meaning as well as offer help, instruction, and reinforcement; and who encourage children to explore and experiment for themselves by providing materials and opportunity. These interactions can be particularly effective when they occur within the context of play. (Bowman 2004, 134)

Why is a climate of acceptance so important? Because preschool and kindergarten children know that they do not write the way that adults do. They are surrounded by print in their lives. Yet when they try to imitate it they run into their own limitations: their fine-motor skills and ability to copy the exact forms of letters are still developing. And their knowledge of letter-sound correspondence and spelling is just emerging. For them, every act of writing is one of taking a risk: Will others make fun of me because I don't write like my parents or older siblings? Teachers have to set up a climate of acceptance in the classroom and make it clear to children that any mark-making attempts they try are welcomed. When they perceive this acceptance, they will take the risk and play with writing and representation more fully.

In my own classrooms, I distinguished the differences between "grown-up writing" and "preschooler and kindergartner writing." At group times, I modeled ways that some preschoolers and kindergartners write with marks, scribble writing, letter-like shapes, random letters, or inventive spelling. And I assured the children that all of these ways of writing were acceptable. At the same time, I talked about how their skills and abilities were going to change over time. As they grew and learned, they would begin to write more like grown-ups.

This discussion was appropriate for three-, four-, and five-year-olds in preschool and kindergarten. There were differences in expectations though, depending on the age of the children. For the younger children, marks, scribble writing, and letter-like shapes were more typically evident in their writing,

while the older preschoolers incorporated more letters, and the kindergartners experimented with more inventive spelling. In all of the preschool and kindergarten settings in which I taught, writing names in a recognizable way was something we worked on daily through sign-in sheets and labeling of paintings, drawings, and other works. Again, for the three-year-olds, "recognizable" might mean a familiar mark or attempts at letter representation of a few of the letters in their names. For the older preschoolers and kindergartners, more accurate representation was possible, so the expectation of progress toward accurate letter representation was present in many classroom activities. However, no matter the age of the children, in play situations it was not expected. In play, any kind of writing was welcomed.

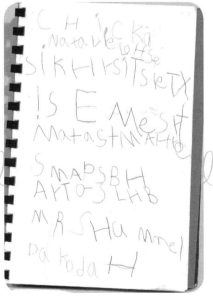

This message of acceptance empowered many children to incorporate more writing into their play experiences. Here's an example of four-year-olds using a variety of writing skills to make tickets for a train trip in their dramatic play:

Making Train Tickets

In a program located in an urban setting, four-year-olds were playing at traveling by train. "We need tickets," they told their teacher, Brian. He helped them find some pieces of construction paper and cut them into 3 x 8½ inch pieces (knowing that this size might guarantee more success at writing than the much smaller size of the actual train tickets). Using markers, seven children gathered at a table near where chairs were set up as a train and began to make tickets. Adrianna did scribble writing that looked like adult cursive, covering the ticket completely. "This tells which room you go to," she said. Jasmine made marks and lines on her ticket. "I'm going to Cincinnati to see my aunt," she said. José and Mario wrote their names so everyone would know that these were their tickets. Shoshanna wrote the numerals 5 and 3. "My seat is number fifty-three. What's yours?" A stop sign was sitting nearby in the dramatic play area. Theo looked at it and copied the word *STOP* onto his ticket. "This says 'stop,'" he said. He still used his ticket to get on the train! All participated with motivation and confidence, happy to be a part of the action and not worried about the reactions of others to their writing.

Beyond providing the materials, Brian's interaction with the children was not necessary for the making of tickets to occur. No child in this particular scenario needed him to provide scaffolding for his or her successful involvement. But this certainly is not always the case. Sometimes scaffolding must be provided by the teacher through interacting and giving reassurance, providing strategies and clues to help children be successful, and offering suggestions for resources that might be helpful. Remember the sand play from chapter 2 where Mary Anne and her colleague had to give the play more focus? As this play continued, they also added representation to deepen it, but had to provide scaffolding for the children in order to help them be successful. Here's what happened:

Sand Play, continued with representation

Mary Anne and her colleague decided that they needed to give the children more clearly defined reasons to dig in the sand. They went to the library and checked out books on archaeology, then read to the children about how animal remains have been found buried in the soil, giving scientists information about life on the earth at different times in the earth's history. They then buried small animal and dinosaur figures in the sand and encouraged the children to carefully dig them up just like the archaeologists in the book had done. They changed the digging tools from shovels and containers to small brushes and spoons, which encouraged more careful digging as well as more use of fine-motor skills. Once the items were found in the sand, they were sorted and categorized by types of animals, sizes, and when they lived, and charts were made to document what was found. A teacher was nearby each day at the "dig site" so that she could help the children sort and document what they found in the sand. (Gronlund and James 2008, 105)

As the children sorted and categorized what they found, Mary Anne asked, "Would you like to draw about what you are doing?" The response was positive, so she added paper and crayons to the mix. Henry immediately wrote his name on his paper and then proceeded to trace over a starfish. "I'm done," he announced. "What did you make?" Mary Anne asked. "A starfish," he said. Mary Anne asked, "Do you want to write the word?" "No," Henry announced and left the table to put his drawing in his cubby. Marissa was drawing a circle with smaller circles inside it. "It's the sand dollar," she told Mary Anne, then asked, "How do you spell sand dollar?" As Mary Anne named each letter, Marissa wrote it across her paper. Some of the letters were backward, some were capitals, and others were lowercase. But the writing was recognizable. Justin scribbled across his paper. "This says 'ocean' I've been to the ocean once." Mary Anne asked if he would like her to write the word *ocean* in grown-up writing. "No, that's okay. I know what it says," Justin replied. Mary Anne said, "You know that book right by you has the word *ocean* right here." She showed him where it was, and Justin spent the next few minutes copying the word. He did not get all of the letters, but he did write the *o, c,* and *n.* Mary Anne said, "Oh, I see you have some of the letters from the book and your own way of writing *ocean*. Way to go, Justin."

Sometimes resources themselves, like the book in the example above, can serve as the scaffold for a child's success in using representation. If children know where to find the information they need to represent what they are trying to draw or write, they may seek it out for themselves and may not need the teacher's assistance. This takes planning on the teacher's part, as well as communication with the children, and is probably more common with older preschoolers and kindergartners than with three-year-olds.

One form of writing that carries great meaning for children at any age is their own name and the names of their classmates. Having cards with the children's names on them around the room may encourage children to find their own name and attempt to write it in play situations. They may even attempt to write a friend's name as well.

Name cards are very beneficial resources when playing at writing letters and delivering mail to the post office. A group of children I taught figured out that they could write their own names on pieces of stationery, fold the pieces up, put them in envelopes, and write their friends' names on the envelopes. They mailed the letters in the class mailbox and when the mail carrier delivered the mail, they could figure out who the recipient was. Once the recipient opened up the letter, she or he could figure out who the sender was. This was a meaningful way to play with using names!

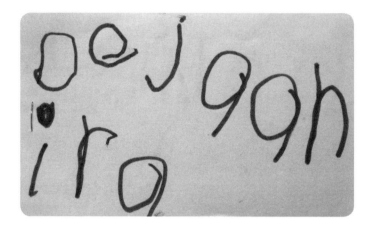

In many classrooms with four- and five-year-old children, teachers post alphabet charts where children can easily see them (at children's eye level is best). These charts contain the letters of the alphabet and familiar objects whose names begin with each letter. In my experience, children will turn to this resource only if a teacher has modeled for them a couple of important steps.

The first step is to demonstrate ways to listen for beginning sounds. Teachers can point out alliteration: "Baby Beluga—those two words start with the same sound, don't they?" And they can give clues for identifying letters by asking questions such as: "What letter does your name start with? What about your friend Megan?" They can also talk through the process of making the connection between letters and sounds when modeling writing. For example, a teacher might say, "Let's see, *train* starts with a 't' sound. Where on the chart do I see something that starts with a 't' sound? Hmmm, here's a truck. Truck. Does that start with the same sound? I think it does—and that letter is *t*. I'm going to write a *t* on my train ticket. How about you? What are you going to write?" By giving these demonstrations, the teacher is making it possible for the chart itself to become scaffolding as children seek to represent their thoughts in writing. Without these preparatory actions, they may not use the chart at all.

Many preschool and kindergarten teachers model writing for children at large- and small-group times. As children speak—giving ideas for a project or class problem or reviewing what they saw on a field trip—a teacher writes their words on a large chart, whiteboard, or chalkboard. In this way, the teacher is demonstrating the connection between oral and written language. Creating word lists or posting words on walls or bulletin boards can be another form of scaffolding children's writing. If the words have meaning for the children and if they participated in choosing the words that are included, they may turn to the lists or wall displays when they are trying to write in their play scenarios. This is a more reasonable and effective strategy for older preschoolers and especially for kindergartners. Younger preschoolers benefit from teachers modeling such writing, but they often do not have the interest or fine-motor capabilities to seek out words that they can copy. Sue Jeffers, a kindergarten teacher at University School of Milwaukee, posts "Wonderful Words" along her alphabet chart for the children. These are words that they request to use in their own writing. Because they are important words to them, they want to make sure they spell them correctly. Throughout the year they build a collection of such words that the children can refer to again and again.

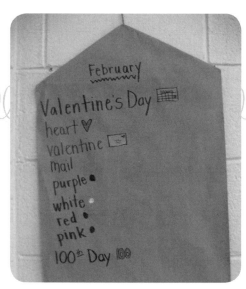

In my teaching days, I discovered a product in an educational supply catalog that was very helpful. I purchased posters of word lists related to interesting topics such as Knights and Castles, Cowboys, and Outer Space. On each poster were approximately fifteen words related to that topic along with pictures of some of the words. This gave me the idea to create more of these posters with the children about the topics they were playing out in dramatic and construction play. We generated these lists together at large-group time. I wrote the words on a piece of chart paper and added pictorial clues as well. I learned a trick from another teacher and fastened the purchased and class-generated posters (all of which I had laminated) on coat hangers and hung them on a rack that the children could easily access. I found the kindergartners were especially interested in using these word lists in both their play and journal writing.

Word walls can also serve the same purpose, but they are not necessarily organized by topics of interest to the children. Even in kindergarten, children do not always have the capability to remember or decode the words posted on a word wall. Another teacher made books of key words organized by topics of interest to the children. For example, a hospital book might contain pictures of a shot, a pill, liquid medicine, and an X-ray and the accompanying

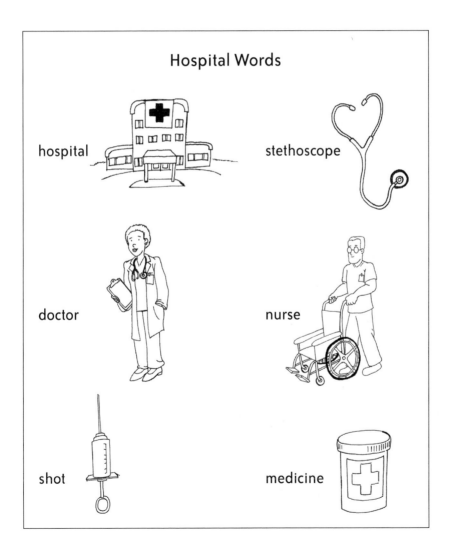

words so children could write them on their prescription pads; and a grocery store book would contain pictures of various food items and their names. The children had a sense of what they would find in each book and could turn to it easily to scaffold their writing as they wrote prescriptions or made grocery lists. With the advent of the Internet, many teachers can now find graphics for the pictures on word lists and books. Providing picture dictionaries for the children can give them another resource to turn to when they want to include writing in their play.

Encourage Mathematical Representation

Throughout this chapter we have discussed adding representation to children's play experience with a focus mostly on drawing and writing. Mathematical representation can also be brought to play to enhance and enrich it. Many of the dramatic play themes, such as grocery store, naturally involve mathematical concepts. Adding the representation of those concepts can easily be done to add another layer of complexity to the play experience.

POSITIONAL WORDS
Children built a structure with 6-8 blocks, represented it on paper, and then described where one block was in the structure using positional words.

Representations often help to make mathematical relationships more obvious. These include common mathematical representations introduced by teachers as well as child-created representations . . .

Children should also learn that representation helps them remember what they did and explain their reasoning. In addition, teachers should often ask children to verbally or concretely represent a concept by showing the number in another way or by using their words and objects to communicate their ideas. (Copley 2000, 44–45)

As with writing in dramatic play, mathematical representation should be encouraged when it makes sense and not added on to change the play into an academic lesson. So if children are making grocery lists, a teacher can ask, "How many eggs will you want to buy?" and encourage the children to represent that either by writing the numeral or drawing the number of eggs they want. If children are building with blocks and measuring their height with measuring tapes, a teacher can invite them to write the height on a chart or sign to share with others. Concerns about who has more or less come up in many aspects of play

as children need to share and take turns with materials. Encouraging them to organize the materials so they can be easily compared and evenly distributed can help solve some disagreements. If many children want to work with the most popular manipulatives, encouraging them to line them up on the table may help them compare how many each person has and divide them more evenly. Providing a timer for sharing can be another positive way to encourage children to resolve these kinds of differences. The passage of time is shown on the face of the timer—a form of mathematical representation used to good purpose.

If children need to write numerals in their play at a shoe store, for example, they may need the teacher's help in scaffolding that writing. Like alphabet charts, number charts displayed in the room can provide that scaffolding as well. Teachers can add mathematical representation in their documentation of children's play as well. Rather than writing a script of the children's play, a teacher can create a graph and share it with the children after the play period ends: "Today I saw three children in the block area, four at the sensory table, five in dramatic play, and three at the art area." Using the children's name cards, teachers can display what they saw in a graph format and introduce data collection and representation to the group.

Representation through photo documentation, dictation, and anecdotes adds validity to children's play. And providing materials and encouragement so children include writing letters, words, and numerals as well as drawing in their play often takes it to more complex levels. The next chapter explores ways to incorporate early learning standards into children's play—not by changing the play, but rather by bringing out the academic experiences and learning opportunities that are imbedded in children's high-quality play.

CHAPTER 8

Incorporating Standards and Goals in Children's Play

> Learning standards and developmentally appropriate practices can indeed
> go together! No change in practices is necessary. Learning standards can
> be incorporated into play, into emergent curriculum and projects, and into
> small and large group times. (Gronlund 2006, 4)

Rosa has seen early learning standards come alive in her mixed-age group of three-, four-, and five-year-olds. She watches and interacts with them as they play, and she is continually amazed at how each child demonstrates progress toward the standards. Some of the children are just beginning to understand concepts or use skills, while others are quite adept at doing so. The standards have helped Rosa figure out materials and experiences that challenge each child in a way that will lead to greater development while also providing a sense of success. The standards give her reasonable expectations and a firm foundation to stand on when she completes an assessment of each child's capabilities.

This chapter looks at ways teachers can incorporate standards and goals into children's play and will challenge the notion that play and standards are somehow mutually exclusive. This chapter offers ideas for how to

- see standards and goals in action
- observe for assessment purposes
- observe to determine next steps
- add challenging and achievable goals to sustain children's interests
- help others see standards and goals through documentation displays

Balancing Play and Standards

Most states in the United States have published early learning standards for three- and four-year-olds as well as for kindergartners. And many are now developing standards for infants and toddlers as well. Early learning standards provide reasonable expectations for young children's development and can guide curriculum planning as well as assessment processes. If used well, they give early educators common language and clear expectations for children's development and "can lead to greater opportunities for positive development and learning in these early years" (NAEYC 2002, 2). However, they can be misused if they interfere with developmentally appropriate practices in preschools and kindergartens. "Thus, a test of the value of any standards effort is whether it promotes positive educational and developmental outcomes and whether it avoids penalizing or excluding children from needed services and supports" (NAEYC 2002, 2).

As discussed throughout this book, play is an essential part of developmentally appropriate practices. Unfortunately, some early educators have taken steps to limit play because they think it takes away from children's opportunities to learn and achieve standards and goals. Sadly, this is especially true in kindergartens across the country: "time for play in most public kindergartens has dwindled to the vanishing point, replaced by lengthy lessons and standardized testing" (Miller and Almon 2009, 2).

The Alliance for Childhood raises serious concerns about the long-term implications of the disappearance of play in kindergarten: "If the problems are not recognized and remedied, the same ills will be passed on to preschools and even to programs for children ages birth to three" (Miller and Almon 2009, 4). And in the NAEYC Position Statement on Developmentally Appropriate Practices, this concern is echoed: "In the high-pressure classroom, children are less likely to develop a love of learning and a sense of their own competence and ability to make choices, and they miss much of the joy and expansive learning of childhood" (Copple and Bredekamp 2009, 4–5).

And yet, play and standards can go together! Preschool and kindergarten teachers around the country incorporate standards and goals into their curricula and do not give up the long time periods necessary for high-level play to develop. Standards do *not* have to be a separate part of the day. They do *not* have to be addressed only in teacher-led small- and large-group times where children are passive learners, required to sit quietly for long periods of time. *Absolutely not!* Instead, standards and curricular goals can be seen in action as children act out dramatic play scenarios, build with blocks, construct with manipulatives, and work with sand and water at the sensory table.

> Planning curriculum with early learning standards in mind does not require a complete change in teaching practices. Providing play, exploration, and active learning opportunities and recognizing the value in daily routines and the importance of caring adults as guides and observers are still the best ways to teach young children. Incorporating standards requires adding a layer of awareness to your planning and implementation so that you can clearly see where standards are being addressed and add ways to bring them more to the forefront. (Gronlund 2006, 16)

Seeing Standards and Goals in Action

Teachers have to become familiar with their state's standards in order to see them in action. They need to know the domains and have a sense of the expectations in each. In most state standards, the domains include language and literacy, mathematics, science, social studies, and approaches to learning; some states also include the social/emotional, physical, and creative domains.

Becoming familiar with standards doesn't necessarily mean memorizing all of them. That would be a tall task indeed! Yet it's important for teachers to have a good sense of what the expectations are. Some teachers display posters with key standards in the classroom to remind themselves of what they are looking for. However, there can be a problem with this strategy. After awhile, teachers may not even see the posters anymore—they have blended into the background and are not an integral part of their daily thinking. Another idea is to post standards, as Marissa did (chapter 1, page 10), by making signs in the various play areas of the classroom to which standards can be affixed with Velcro.

The Velcro allows the standards to be changed. As teachers think about addressing standards while children play, they change the signs to remind themselves of their goals for various play activities. Teachers report that this process really helps them get to know the standards better, incorporate them into their lesson plans, and see them more fully in action.

Understanding Standards in Natural and Intentional Ways

There are two ways to see standards in action in preschool and kindergarten classrooms:

- teachers can see them happening *naturally* throughout all of the activities in a typical day
- they can plan to bring them about *intentionally* in a variety of activities

When teachers lead large- and small-group activities, it may be easy to see standards occurring naturally in the classroom. For example, it's probably obvious that children are working on language and literacy standards when they are listening to a story, making predictions that show their comprehension, asking about unfamiliar vocabulary words, or connecting familiar alphabet letters or words to their own experiences (For example, "Look, that's a *J* like in Justin's name!"). Much of the time, standards are being addressed in play as well. When teachers observe play with that focus, they see standards happening all the time. The following story is from a preschool classroom:

Standards in Dramatic Play

In Lisa and Roseanne's classroom of four-year-olds, two girls, Hannah and Ling, played in the dramatic play area for approximately twenty-five minutes. Lisa observed them as they tried on various hats, dresses, capes, and shoes and looked at themselves often in the mirror. At one point, Ling was wearing a crown of flowers. Hannah tugged the crown off of Ling's head. Ling smiled, fixed her hair, and did not protest. She just got another hat. Then Hannah found a plastic lunch box. She opened it up and started to put play food items in it. Ling went to the play refrigerator and passed food items to Hannah, announcing what each one was as she did so. "Apple, orange, banana, hot dog," said Ling. As Hannah put the hot dog in the lunch box, she said, "No, that's not a fruit," and took it out.

Lisa and Roseanne met after the morning session for a few minutes before heading to lunch. Lisa told Roseanne about the scene she had witnessed with the girls. As they talked, they realized that many early learning standards had been addressed in the play. Together, they made a list of standards, which included

- using language to converse
- dressing and undressing self
- playing and cooperating with another child
- getting along with a friend without conflict (for Ling)
- sorting and categorizing (for Hannah)
  (Gronlund 2006, 12)

To see standards occurring naturally in children's play, teachers need to be familiar with the standards, observe children carefully, and reflect on what they observed. Discussing with a colleague, as Lisa and Roseanne did, can help, and looking through the standards themselves while talking about what the children did will add to the discussion. Notice that the standards identified for Hannah and Ling crossed several domains. They were not just in the social/emotional domain. In their play, the girls also used language, fine-motor, and self-help skills, and for Hannah, mathematical thinking. This is typical in children's high-level play—they integrate many skills and understandings. What a rich place for teachers to see standards in action!

Here's another example of standards occurring in a natural way in my own kindergarten classroom:

Dinosaur March

Dinosaurs were intriguing to many of the children in my classroom. They played with plastic dinosaur figures, incorporating them into block constructions and creating dramatic play scenarios with them. They read the dinosaur books in the library and drew pictures and wrote about dinosaurs in their journals. I found a big book called *Dinosaur March*. It contained a song with a simple melody and a strong beat. I introduced it to the children at a large-group time. It quickly became a favorite song to sing, and we usually marched vigorously around the room as we sang the names of the many types of dinosaurs in the song.

I felt it was important to give children access to the words to songs, so I had them displayed near the group time area. The children knew where to find the Class Songbook and other resources that we used during group time. And the *Dinosaur March* book was available as well. One day, Spencer took the book back to the dramatic play area. He laid the book open on the table and began to sing as he looked at each page, accurately reciting the words to the song and turning the pages appropriately as he did so. Soon, several other children joined him. Stephanie said, "We have to march like the dinosaurs," and organized the group into a line with Spencer at the head with the book in hand. He held up each page as the group sang and marched, but when it came time to turn the page, the group stopped and waited patiently for him to get to the next page so they could sing that line of the song. They had a clear connection to the print on the page and did not march forward until they could see the words and pictures that went with what they were singing. Stephanie then suggested to the group that they each take a turn as the "Dinosaur Leader" and they did. This marching and singing went on for over twenty minutes with six children participating both as marchers and song leaders.

I saw many kindergarten standards evident in this playful, child-initiated activity. For all six of the children involved, I saw their awareness that print carries a message that is constant. They used memory to recite the song and vocabulary to identify the dinosaurs. Spencer and the other leaders used picture and context clues to know when to turn the pages. And Stephanie showed leadership and planning skills. All six engaged in a cooperative activity, sharing and taking turns.

These stories illustrate the need for teachers to set up the conditions that bring about high-level play, for it is in such play that so many of the standards and curricular goals are seen. In high-level play, children stretch themselves. "In the long term, higher order play among preschoolers primarily evolves into imaginative, creative, abstract, and divergent thinking and expression. . . . Higher order play leads to higher order thinking" (Saifer 2009, 15). So, if teachers do not support play that moves beyond the chaotic or simplistic, they will not be able to bring about as much growth in the children's performances related to state standards and curricular goals. Doing away with play periods and substituting teacher-led, skill-based activities is not the way to reach higher standards. Instead, facilitating high-level play is the way!

Teachers can be intentional when incorporating standards into play. When teachers post their goals with Velcro on the area signs, they are intentionally identifying which standards they will look for as children play in those areas. They are also reminding themselves that the materials they provide in each area and the open-ended questions they ask children as they play can focus on the standards they've selected. Here's an example of teachers intentionally incorporating early learning standards in play in a preschool classroom:

King and Queen Reader

Robin and Whitney teach three-year-olds. In their early learning standards, they noted that interest in books and book-handling skills, such as holding the book correctly, turning one page at a time, and scanning from left to right, were included. They already had a library area in their room and had noticed that various children went over there during Activity Time. Robin suggested that they make this area a little more enticing so that they could really focus on children's skills in relation to this standard. Whitney suggested that they take the crown and cape out of the dress-up area and place them in the library on a special chair. Then any child who wished could go to the library area and be the "King or Queen Reader." They agreed that they would need to take turns observing who chose to join in this activity and then make notes about that child's book-handling skills.

When they introduced the idea of King and Queen Readers to the children, they immediately had several enthusiastic volunteers, so many that they had to make a waiting list of the children's names to ensure that everyone would get a chance. As Whitney or Robin observed each child, they took brief notes about the child's handling of the book and awareness of the reading process. Luke held the book appropriately and made up his own story, which was not related to the actual book at all. He occasionally turned the pages, sometimes from front to back and sometimes from back to front. Mario also held the book appropriately and carefully studied each picture, making up a story that was related to what he saw in each picture, turning pages one at a time. Anika chose a book with which she was very familiar. She held the book in front of her as a teacher would do, showing the other children gathered around. Her eyes scanned the pages from left to right, and occasionally, her finger pointed along under the words on the page as she recounted the story accurately, almost word for word. By setting up this activity, Robin and Whitney learned much about how each child was progressing in his or her book handling and early reading skills. (Gronlund 2006, 13)

These teachers addressed early learning standards within a child-initiated, playful activity by adding materials and ideas for play. The children were already going to the reading area. Now they had a special costume and role to play as they read. How engaging for them! In addition, each child's capabilities with reading were accepted and validated. Telling your own story, telling one from the pictures, or reciting the book from memory were all valued and celebrated. And each child gave Robin and Whitney a clear idea of his or her understanding of the reading process.

Enhancing Play to Incorporate Standards

When teachers support and enhance play in all of the ways that have been explored in this book, they can also incorporate early learning standards. It's not necessary to set up only teacher-led activities to do so. Teachers can be intentional by putting together specific materials or activities to address standards as in the above scenario, or intentional by asking questions within well-timed interventions in children's play as in the following example from a kindergarten classroom:

Blocks and Measuring Tapes

Two boys, Luis and Matthew, were building in the block area. Luis had a measuring tape hanging over his shoulders. Matthew enclosed a space with layers of long wooden blocks. "This is for the lions so they can't get out," Matthew said. Luis passed more blocks to Matthew as he stacked, then started building a low wall off to the side of the lions' cage. "Look, Matt, this is gonna be really long," Luis said. Their teacher, Tina, was sitting on the floor nearby. Luis said, "Look, Tina, this is the road so the guys can bring the food to the lions." Tina replied, "That is a long road, Luis. And I see you have your measuring tape. Are you going to measure it to see how long it is?" Luis took the measuring tape off his shoulders and laid it down along the road. "Thirty-four!" he called out. "How did you know it was thirty-four?" Tina asked. "I just know," Luis answered. "How about we lay it down with the number one at this end and hold it straight?" Tina suggested. Together they pulled the measuring tape taut and looked at the number at the other end of the road. "Twenty-six! Hey, Matt, it's twenty-six!" Luis said. "Come do this one," Matt said, pointing to the wall of his lion cage. "Where will the end go when you measure up and down instead of on the floor?" Tina asked. Again, she assisted as they figured out the best way to measure. Several other structures were built and measured. And Tina suggested that the boys might like to label those structures with their lengths and heights. They created signs with the numerals on them and taped them to each of the structures. "How do you write *inches*?" Luis asked and wrote the letters as Tina spelled them out for him.

"I want to write 'Watch out for the lions!'" Matthew said, and Tina helped him figure out the letters needed for his sign as well.

Tina's facilitation of this play led to both boys using many skills tied to kindergarten standards. Her well-timed questions and assistance enabled them to use a measuring tool, problem solve, and represent mathematical information as well as words and messages.

In both of the examples of intentionality above, the teachers did not change the play experience into an academic lesson led by the teacher. Instead, they incorporated academic learning into the children's play interests. Whether seeing standards and goals naturally in children's play, or taking steps to intentionally bring them out in play, teachers are still working to facilitate, support, and deepen the play experience for children, not to interrupt it with on-demand tasks that do not sustain what the children are doing. There are other parts of the daily schedule that can be devoted to teacher-led small-group activities that are more focused on such tasks. When the time period allotted for play is protected and valued, teachers will see standards, goals, and academic learning as children apply them in their high-level play experiences.

Observe for Assessment Purposes

Paying attention to children's play then becomes part of the assessment process. Play is a prime time to observe for children's progress toward standards and goals. "Documenting children's progress toward achieving standards and benchmarks should be done in ways that are developmentally appropriate. . . . When we know what children can do on their own, we can use . . . standards to help us determine what additional skills we can work on to help them progress in their development" (Jacobs and Crowley 2007, 9). Throughout this book, the many ways for teachers to be intentional as they support and enhance children's play have been explored. When integrated with a teacher's knowledge of standards and curricular goals, these teacher actions can also be ways to assess how each child is progressing in relation to those standards and goals.

One of the reasons that teachers can observe so many early learning standards when children are engaged in high-level play is that children often combine types of play. Steffen Saifer (2009, 14) has developed a new conceptualization of play in development. He proposes that preschoolers and kindergartners often combine creative, complex play with skill-based play. He says that skill-based play "emerges from functional, practical play and motor activities, such as running, chasing, climbing, tricycle/bicycle riding, doing puzzles, engaging in simple games, and the like."

In skill-based play, children are exercising their mental skills and their muscles, and in creative, complex play, they engage primarily their thinking and imagination. Observant teachers see this in action and can make the connection to the skills and expectations identified in early learning standards. Here's an example of a child combining the types of play:

> A child starts building a house with plastic interlocking construction blocks by following a diagram, but after awhile, follows her own ideas for building a house. Soon a friend joins and they decide to work together to turn it into a spaceship. (Saifer 2009, 14–15)

Upon observing this scenario, a teacher could identify the following standards that were addressed as the child used both skill-based and creative, complex play:

- uses eye-hand coordination with small manipulatives
- demonstrates curiosity, initiative, self-direction, and persistence
- works cooperatively with other children
- uses materials in creative ways to represent other objects

By observing the play and writing down a description of what the child did, the teacher is collecting documentation to use for evaluating the child's progress. Teachers can also add a photograph of the child's creation, or a photo of the two friends at work. They could ask questions as the children work and note important aspects of the conversation.

All of this documentation, then, helps teachers make the connection to the standards as they reflect about what they saw and heard. Teachers can record the standards identified on a checklist or portfolio form and assign a level or rating that shows where the child is performing in relation to that standard. In many preschool and kindergarten programs, teachers use checklists and report forms that are based on the state's early learning standards or tied to a particular curriculum. Documentation, such as observation or anecdotal notes, photographs, and work samples, is also collected in portfolios to provide the evidence to support the ratings and evaluations given on progress reports. This is authentic assessment—the combination of collecting documentation as children engage in a variety of activities including play, and evaluating how the child is doing based on the accepted criteria of state standards and curricular goals.

"Standards provide us with a *path*, a direction that guides our teaching and what children are learning. They should not be viewed as a pass/fail measurement. It is important that we keep in mind that our goal is to help children develop and grow in their understandings, not merely be able to repeat information back to us" (Jacobs and Crowley 2007, 132). Play that develops into productive, high-level play is an authentic activity, rich in information about how children are growing and developing.

Observe to Determine Next Steps

The assessment process also includes determining next steps for each child. Teachers review their documentation, consider the child's progress related to standards, and ask themselves: What is she ready for? What challenging and achievable goals can I consider for her? And what curricular plans will best meet her where she is and help her to move on in progress and accomplishments? All of these questions can be related to play experiences. The answers to them will determine what the teacher will do to support and enhance this child's play experience.

> Assessment information is vital to guide teachers' planning. The excellent teacher uses her observations and other information gathered to inform her planning and teaching, giving careful consideration to the learning experiences needed by the group as a whole and by each individual child. By observing what children explore, what draws their interest, and what they say and do, the teacher determines how to adapt the environment, materials, or daily routines. The teacher can make an activity simpler or more complex according to what individual children are ready for. Then, her follow-up plans can include giving children repeated experiences with an idea or skills to get a solid grasp of it. Effective planning also means considering where the child or group of children might go next. (Copple and Bredekamp 2009, 44–45)

Here's an example of a teaching team using the planning process to review their observations of children and consider where to go next:

Separation and Independence

In their group of older two-year-olds and younger three-year-olds, Joan and Steve often deal with separation difficulties. Children cry, cling to their parents, and take awhile to get started in activities in the classroom. Joan and Steve are very sensitive to this process and have done many things to help both parents and children. Mothers and fathers are encouraged to stay with their children for the first couple of weeks and to linger as needed after that. Cues are given to parents when children are actively engaged and ready to say good-bye. However, after several weeks had passed, Joan and Steve noticed that Sharie was still taking a long time to ease into the classroom. Steve observed her arrival and wrote down the following anecdote one day:

"Grrrr, grrrrr." From the doorway between the cubby room and the classroom, a dry, raspy growl is heard. *"Grrrrr, grrrrrr."*

Three-year-old Sharie steps into the classroom followed by her mother. Sharie's stance is tense and wide, braced for action. Her arms are outstretched. Her hands and fingers are scrunched up as claws. With teeth bared, Sharie gives another growling greeting to the teacher while clawing the air. Approaching the teacher, she stomps down hard with each step.

Sharie continues to growl and flex her claws. Then she turns to the mirror and growls at her image. (Klein, Wirth, and Linas 2004)

The two teachers discussed what they might do and Joan came up with an idea. "Maybe she wants to be a lion and we could go along with that play idea to ease her into the room." So, the next day they greeted the growling Sharie with, "Welcome to the lion's den. All of the other lions are here. *Growl, growl.* See them playing over there. Here's a blanket for the lion to have at school if she wants. Some of the lions carry them around so they can have something warm and cuddly." Sharie's eyes lit up as the teachers growled with her. She took the blanket, hugged her mom, and went readily with Joan. This continued for several days.

Joan and Steve introduced another play activity that helped Sharie and her classmates with separation. They encouraged children to dress up as Mommies and Daddies and made cars out of chairs so that the children could drive away. "Good-bye. Good-bye, Mommy," Steve would call out. Some children would leave again and again.

Most early learning standards include something under the social/emotional or approaches to learning domain about developing independence. In this case, these teachers were working with that expectation in its early development—separating from familiar adults. Knowing that an expectation is identified for later development helps guide teachers' decision making as they plan for play experiences that help them work toward standards. Rather than apply the expectations designated as appropriate for four-year-olds turning five, teachers of younger children look at those expectations and identify the first steps a child might make toward those expectations as in the separation example above.

Here's another example of a teacher reflecting on what she has observed in her kindergarten children's play and how she figured out the appropriate next steps to help them be successful:

The Chase Game

In Mrs. Taylor's kindergarten classroom, "chase" was a very popular game to play outdoors. Usually, the boys chased the girls and the girls ran away from them, screaming loudly. If they were caught, the girls called to Mrs. Taylor for help. She often intervened, reminding the boys to be gentle and to release the girls from their grasp. Then, as she turned her back, the chase game began again. Mrs. Taylor was worried about the repetition involved, the aggressiveness of the boys toward the girls, and the girls' lack of assertiveness in the whole experience. What could she do?

She decided to ask the children what they thought and brought up the topic at the next group meeting time. She invited children to share their perspectives on why the chase game was fun or not fun for them, and she recorded their thoughts on chart paper. Then she asked them to do some hard thinking about ways they could change the game so it might be more fun for all involved. She suggested they all think about ideas overnight and come back tomorrow for a further discussion.

She was delighted to hear many suggestions from the children the next day. She welcomed everyone's input as they discussed the benefits and drawbacks of each idea. And she led them in a voting process so they could decide on one idea to try for that day's time outdoors. The majority voted in favor of Tanesha's idea that they write on the whiteboard before each recess time who got to chase whom: girls or boys. Tanesha, a good writer, nominated herself to make the decision and do the writing each time. And much to Mrs. Taylor's surprise, all in the group went along with that suggestion. So, as children prepared to go outdoors that morning, Tanesha loudly called out as she wrote on the board, "Girls chase today!" And they did. Boys screamed and laughed as the girls chased after them. The game became more of a game of "tag" than "capture." For several days, the boys and girls rotated roles of pursuer and pursued. Then, Mrs. Taylor wondered if both boys and girls could chase sometimes. More discussions ensued, votes were taken, new recorders were found, and the play changed again, still maintaining a more positive outcome than earlier.

Observing children at play, asking questions in reflection, and even inviting the children to participate in such reflection can have very positive benefits for all involved.

Add Challenging and Achievable Goals to Sustain Children's Interest

Most young children relish a challenge. Developmentally, they are continually adding new skills and capabilities to their repertoire and are motivated to continue to do so. When children feel safe and cared for and are playing in a climate of trust and community, they will seek out opportunities to try something new, something hard. And they will respond to a trusted teacher's suggestions for new challenges for them—challenges that are at the right level for them to stretch their abilities without being overwhelming or too difficult.

Challenging children by asking well-timed and open-ended questions can make children think more fully about what they are doing. By providing new and provocative materials or adding representation, teachers can help children take their play to more complicated levels. I have had great success in suggesting challenges to preschool and kindergarten children as they play by asking a simple but attention-getting question: "Would you like a challenge over here?" I only do so if I see that their play could use an infusion of something different. It may have been at a high level, but it seems to be slipping into simplistic or chaotic play, or the children are losing interest in it. Often, children respond enthusiastically to my query: "Sure!" The challenges I offer, then, need to be engaging, interesting, and at a level just above what the children were doing. I have to know the children well in order to determine that level. Then I need to be available to get them started and assess if I did choose a challenge at the right level for them. If necessary, I'll make adjustments depending on the results.

Here's an example of a teacher, Jeff, offering a challenge to children:

Blocks, Ramps, and Friction

In his preschool classroom, Jeff noticed that the children's block play was not quite as complex as it had been in the past. He had taught the children how to make ramps with the blocks and watched them as they rolled cylindrical blocks and various small vehicles down them. But they didn't seem to know what else to do at that point, and only a few children remained with the activity for any length of time. Jeff decided to introduce a challenge at the block area and see whether that might bring about higher levels of engagement.

As he introduced the play areas and activities the next day, he posed this question to the group: "In the block area today, I have a challenge for you. If we changed the surface of the ramps you've been building, I wonder if that will change how far and fast things roll down your ramps? I'll need people who are interested in this challenge to choose blocks and come see what materials I have to challenge your thinking." At the block area, he helped the children get two ramps built quickly. Then he showed them the following items: aluminum foil, a carpet mat, a large piece of sandpaper, and a piece of satin fabric. Jeff said, "My challenge to you is: what do you think will happen if we place these different textures on the ramps? Will our blocks and cars roll faster and farther? Or slower and not as far?" The children felt the textures, made predictions, and conducted experiments to see what would happen. Jeff was able to keep this challenge going throughout the week so that all of the children who were interested in participating had an opportunity to do so. He helped them throughout and even kept a chart recording their findings.

Challenges are a way to incorporate the skill-based play that Steffen Saifer (2009) identifies. They help children move up the Hierarchy of Needs toward self-actualization because a good challenge engages children's intellect and problem-solving skills. Principle 11 of the DAP Statement states: "Development and learning advance when children are challenged to achieve at a level just beyond their current mastery, and also when they have many opportunities to practice newly acquired skills" (Copple and Bredekamp 2009, 15).

Challenges can incorporate early learning standards and curricular goals. In the example above, the children had to use many skills and competencies across a variety of domains. It was also important that the teacher remained available to players after offering a challenge because, if he chose well, he identified something just beyond the comfort level of these children. He was there to provide support, make suggestions, and scaffold what they were doing. He was helping them to function in their zone of proximal development (also called ZPD) where Vygotsky and his followers believe learning takes place (Berk and Winsler 1995).

Figuring out the right amount of challenge is essential to making this strategy a worthwhile one. In the new DAP, setting challenging and achievable goals is recommended: "Learning and development are most likely to occur when new experiences build on what a child already knows and is able to do and when those learning experiences also entail the child stretching a reasonable amount in acquiring new skills, abilities, or knowledge" (Copple and Bredekamp 2009, 10).

If children are over-challenged, they may give up in frustration or withdraw. And if they are under-challenged, their behavior may deteriorate and their play becomes out of control. Or they may just withdraw and choose to play elsewhere. Teachers have to know the children well as individuals. What is each child's tolerance of frustration? How does each child tend to go about tasks that are hard? Then, teachers have to watch carefully for responses to their challenges and provide the scaffolding discussed above. If teachers see that the challenge is not an appropriate one, they make adjustments or go in a different direction altogether. This is the art of teaching and the art of facilitating play—a complex process indeed!

Help Others See Standards and Goals through Documentation Displays

Chapter 7 included a discussion on how teachers can create documentation displays to enrich children's play and share it with others. Such displays can also be a way to show the standards and goals addressed in play. Incorporating learning standards into such displays is not difficult. Teachers can add labels to the display that identify the standards or curricular goals that are being addressed. Or they can create a list that accompanies the display with a heading, "Here's what we are learning" and put the standards addressed on it.

Many teachers have found that they can use bulletin boards and newsletters to show the value of play as a vehicle for learning. They include photographs and quotes from the children, explanations of the play process, and connections to standards and goals. In fact, anything that is displayed in a classroom can have an additional label that adds the standard or goal to it. This makes learning come alive for others who may not understand the power of play. Some examples are pictured here.

When we participate in pretend play, we are expanding our expressive language and social skills as we give and follow directions.

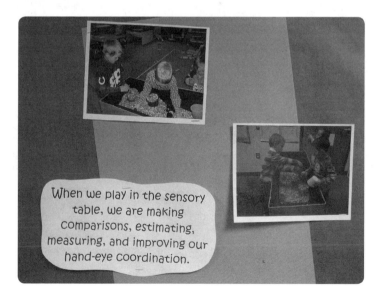

When we play in the sensory table, we are making comparisons, estimating, measuring, and improving our hand-eye coordination.

These are ways to share the value of play with those who may not understand. In showing the integration of learning standards and goals, teachers help parents, administrators, and community members see that they are facilitating children's play experiences so that they are not just *any* experiences, but productive, high-level ones that challenge children to reach their full potential.

Standards and play do indeed go together! Whether teachers plan intentionally to incorporate standards, or observe carefully for their natural integration, they can find that the value of high-level play includes the many skills and concepts imbedded in their state's early learning standards. The concluding chapter summarizes key points about the importance of play for preschool and kindergarten teachers and the important roles that teachers have in facilitating and enhancing rich play experiences.

Conclusion: Play Works

> Every child deserves a chance to grow and learn in a play-based, experiential preschool and kindergarten. Play works. (Miller and Almon 2009, 6)

"Play: Where Learning Begins" was the theme of the National Association for the Education of Young Children's 18th National Institute for Early Childhood Professional Development held in Charlotte, North Carolina, in June 2009. All of the workshops, keynotes, and panel discussions focused on the many aspects of play and its benefits for young children. This focus was timely—with the release of the new DAP, practitioners and leaders in early childhood education were reminded of the importance of play in best practices. And the conversations sparked at the conference were intense and inspiring.

As I look back at my notes from the sessions I attended (and I certainly did not attend all of them), a few key thoughts stand out.

In his keynote address, brain researcher John Medina informed us of the brain's functions: to solve problems related to surviving in an outdoor setting while in constant motion—in other words, to PLAY! He talked about the value of improvisation as part of the learning process and the importance of repetition in order to incorporate and remember new ideas. Children are certainly improvising during play, aren't they? And the repetition of common themes and actions is there as well.

Richard Cohen, an early childhood teacher and consultant, talked about "the spirit of play" and reminded us that young children live in the present.

Because they focus on the moment, the process of play and creation is more important to them than the product that results. This is such a hard concept for early educators to get across to parents and community members. They want to see a product and don't always understand and value the incredible processes involved in high-level, imaginative play.

Well-known play advocate Walter Drew suggested that early educators help children discover their own capacity to create harmony and order in their lives. He sees play as the means to do just that. In high-level play, children behave in much more harmony because they want the play to continue. They stretch themselves, resolve their conflicts more readily, and create an orderly world of their own.

Elena Bodrova and Deborah Leong, authors, researchers, and proponents of the Vygotskian approach to play, pointed out that there is a false dichotomy created when people consider promoting play as antithetical to teaching academic skills. Instead, they heartily endorse that the two go hand in hand. Whether goals are based on early learning standards or on a curricular approach, teachers can incorporate them in children's play. And children can practice many academic skills as they play, especially if teachers provide materials and suggestions for representation through writing and use of numerals.

Along those lines, Ellen Frede, co-director of the National Institute for Early Education Research (NIEER), spoke of a false dilemma when teachers ask, "If the children play, when do I assess?" thinking that assessment cannot take place as children play. As was discussed in earlier chapters, this certainly is not the case—children demonstrate so much as teachers observe them in high-level play experiences. And to be truly authentic, assessment practices should be imbedded in all that children do throughout the day, including long periods of high-level play.

Steffen Saifer of the Northwest Regional Educational Laboratory quoted Albert Einstein: "Imagination is more important than knowledge." And he ended his session with the reminder, "The work of teachers is children's play."

Finally, in the session that I presented with Marlyn James—my coauthor on two previous books and early childhood faculty member at Flathead Valley Community College—entitled "Intentionality and Play in the New DAP," the group of attendees developed the following web in response to our question, "What can teachers do to bring about high-level play?" Their responses and

suggestions closely mirror the many conditions and teacher actions that I have identified in this book. It's refreshing to hear that so many of our fellow early childhood professionals see these conditions as essential in bringing about high-level play for children. Those suggestions have helped to set the path of this book, and I am grateful to these educators for their input.

Not Just Any Play

Developmentally appropriate play is not just *any* play. Teachers in preschools and kindergartens work very hard to plan for play that is enriching and beneficial for the children. They step in and out of play experiences to help children sustain high-quality play, and they challenge children with provocations, integration of standards and goals, and representation. I strongly believe that teachers have an important and vital role in children's play—helping it to be all that it can be!

Suggested Provocations

For Younger Preschoolers and Less-Experienced Players

For Dramatic Play

- Provide prop boxes with appropriate materials for a variety of settings (veterinary office, train station, beauty salon, and others).
- Discuss the various roles people have in those settings and the actions they take in those roles.
- Take a field trip to explore the setting, or plan for a visit by a veterinarian, hairdresser, or others.
- Model ways of acting in this setting—coplay as the veterinarian, the train conductor, or the person getting a haircut.
- Be ready to support the play with language, materials, and other forms of facilitation.
- Encourage children to find what they need in other parts of the classroom to support their scenarios (blocks, manipulatives, books, paper, writing tools).

For Construction Play with Both Blocks and Manipulatives

- Add books about houses, bridges, and buildings from around the world to the block area.

- Add vehicles and traffic signs to encourage building of roads and ramps.
- Add animal figures to encourage building of farms and zoos.
- Encourage children to combine their dramatic and construction play by asking questions—for example, "Can you build a fire truck out of blocks for the firefighters?"
- Encourage children to find what they need in other parts of the classroom to support their constructions (manipulatives, books, paper, writing tools).
- Provide photos of a variety of vehicles in the manipulatives area.
- Encourage cross usage of manipulatives—for example, small, colored bears could ride on vehicles made of Duplos; shelters for small animal or dinosaur figures could be made from colored pattern blocks.

At the Sensory Table

Sand or water can be replaced with items with different textures, such as

- air bubble packing and toy hammers
- cotton balls and sandpaper
- potting soil and shovels, with plastic insects for burying and hiding
- colorful foam shapes, with tongs and various cups and bowls
- shredded paper, with shovels and various cups and bowls
- rocks and pebbles, with different types of brushes for cleaning and shining along with drying racks

For Older Preschoolers and Kindergartners

For Dramatic Play

- Provide open-ended or unstructured materials that could be used in many ways to accompany play themes (colorful pieces of fabrics in varying textures and sizes; small boxes and containers that can be substituted for phones and other items; cardboard and plastic tubes for telescopes, swords, and fire hoses).

- Encourage children to make needed props from materials in the classroom (wooden blocks to build a fire for camping; small boxes decorated as walkie-talkies; cardboard tubes as flashlights) or to simply pretend they have the prop they need (an even higher level of symbolic representation).

- As with younger children, expand children's repertoire of play themes beyond their everyday experiences through ongoing studies that build in depth and include field trips, special visitors, and a variety of experiences to represent what is learned (webbing, experience stories, dramatic play materials, and constructions).

- Read a variety of interesting stories and nonfictional books and encourage children to incorporate them in their play; then encourage them to cross characters and plot aspects between stories (for example, "Could the big bad wolf show up when Goldilocks is sleeping in baby bear's bed?").

- Invite children to plan their play beforehand, identifying the play theme, characters, assignment of roles, and actions they will take.

- Encourage children to find what they need in other parts of the classroom to support their scenarios (blocks, manipulatives, books, paper, writing tools).

- Document children's dramatic play through photographs, and record their reflections and retelling of the story they acted out; display and share with others.

For Construction Play with Both Blocks and Manipulatives

- In addition to offering books about houses, buildings, and bridges, include actual architects' plans and developers' blueprints.

- Introduce children to the roles of developer, architect, builder, and inspector and encourage them to play those roles when constructing.

- Add measuring tapes, yardsticks, and rulers to the block area.

- Place a large, blue piece of cloth or paper that's cut in the shape of a lake in the block area and challenge the children to incorporate it into their building.

- Encourage the building of ramps for vehicles to roll down; do a variety of experiments with them (measure how far different vehicles or balls will go, changing the angle of the ramp and comparing the distances; cover the ramp with different materials, such as foil, sandpaper, air bubble packing, or fabric, to see what happens to the distances the objects will roll).

- Invite children to draw the things they built with blocks or manipulatives.

- Encourage children to combine their dramatic and construction play by asking questions—for example, "Can you build a fire truck out of blocks for the firefighters?"

- Encourage children to find what they need in other parts of the classroom to support their constructions (manipulatives, books, paper, writing tools).

- Take photographs of either block or manipulative constructions and invite the children to dictate documentation about their process; then display the documentation to share with others.

- Challenge children to plan their constructions from blocks or Legos before they build them.

- Challenge children to figure out various ways to sort the manipulatives (mixing buttons, bears, Legos, and other items).

At the Sensory Table

Here are some ideas for provocations with sand and water as well as with other materials:

- Hide items (shells, bones, rocks with fossils) in the sand and encourage the children as "paleontologists" to carefully dig for them with shovels, dust them off with small brushes, catalog them (have foam trays and paper and markers for labeling), and analyze them (perhaps with a magnifying glass or microscope).

- Provide construction hats and goggles along with construction vehicles (such as bulldozers) and wooden blocks so children can play at construction in the sand. Encourage planning the site, determining who will move the sand, and deciding who will build the building.

- Provide large milk jugs for filling with water using a variety of sizes of cups, funnels, turkey basters, and eyedroppers; poke a hole in the side of the milk jug, put in a straw, and see how many cups of water need to be poured into the jug before water begins to drip out through the straw.

- Instead of filling the sensory table with water, put two plastic bins in the table—one filled with water, the other empty. Include turkey basters, eyedroppers, hoses, funnels, and measuring cups, and challenge the children to figure out ways to move water to the empty tub.

- Place a large chunk of ice in an empty sensory table along with small cups of colored water. Invite children to fill eyedroppers with colored water and squeeze it onto the chunk of ice to make colorful combinations. In addition, sprinkle salt on the ice and notice what happens. Chronicling how long it takes for the large block to melt may also be of interest.

- Place any of the following materials in an empty sensory table and see what the children construct: beads, pipe cleaners, string, yarn, pieces of drinking straws (cut into different sizes), and lacing wire.

(Ideas adapted from a presentation by Jill Schwartz at NAEYC 2008, Dallas.)

Ideas for Writing Materials to Accompany Dramatic Play

Themes

A Family Home

- a variety of writing tools, including pencils, pens, and markers
- stationery, cards, and envelopes for letter writing; stickers for stamps
- scrap paper or tablets for making grocery lists; grocery circulars from the newspaper for copying; or make a template grocery list as shown on the next page
- scrap paper or tablets placed near the play telephone for taking messages; a class phone book with children's actual or pretend phone numbers listed there
- index cards for writing recipes (place cookbooks nearby)
- checkbooks for paying bills
- calendars for keeping appointments

A Doctor's Office, Veterinarian's Office, or Hospital

- a variety of writing tools, including pencils, pens, and markers
- scrap paper or tablets to be used as prescription pads; or use the sample pad shown below
- scrap paper or tablets on clipboards to be used as patient records; add a file box with file folders—one labeled for each child—to keep each child's records
- calendars or appointment books for scheduling appointments

Prescription

Patient's name _____

Date _____

Take _____ teaspoons or tablets

every _____ hours

Doctor's name _____

A Grocery Store

- a variety of writing tools, including pencils, pens, and markers
- scrap paper or tablets to be used for labeling shelves and aisles; grocery circulars to guide children's labeling process
- scrap paper or tablets to be used for grocery lists; or make a template grocery list as shown on the previous page
- cards to be made into credit cards, checkbooks for writing checks, and paper for making pretend money

From *Developmentally Appropriate Play* by Gaye Gronlund, © 2010.
Redleaf Press grants permission to photocopy this page for classroom use.

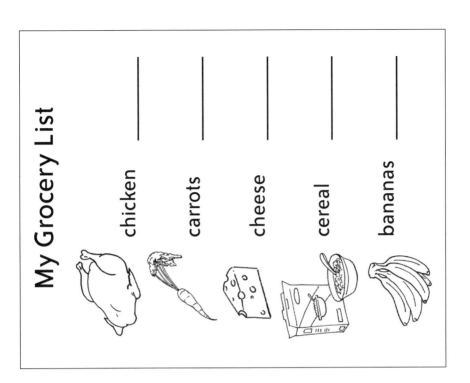

My Grocery List

chicken _____

carrots _____

cheese _____

cereal _____

bananas _____

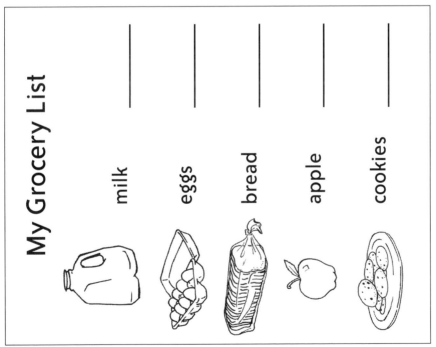

My Grocery List

milk _____

eggs _____

bread _____

apple _____

cookies _____

My Train Ticket

Name _____

To _____

Seat number _____

My Airplane Ticket

Name _____

To _____

Seat number _____

My Bus Ticket

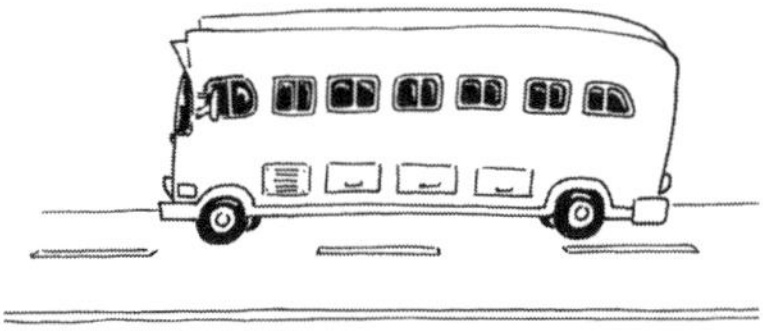

Name _____

To _____

Seat number _____

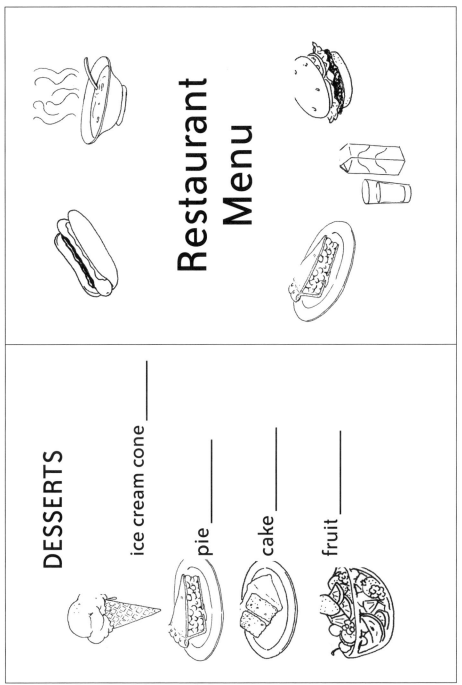

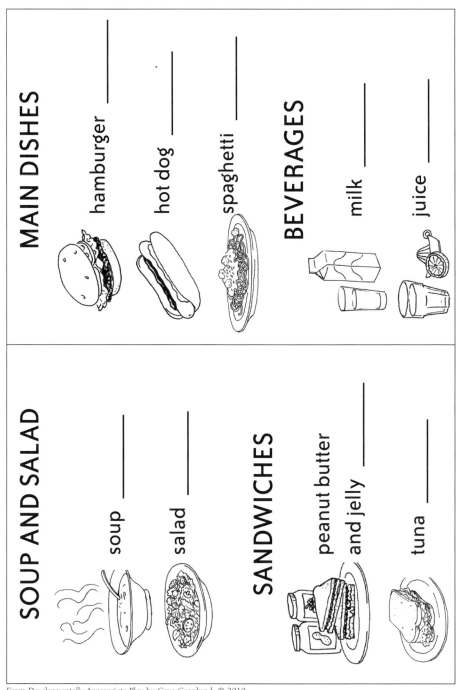

Restaurant Guest Check

Table Number	Number of Persons	Server Number

Quantity	Item	Cost
	TOTAL	

Library

My Library Card

My name

_____

My Library
Checkout Record

My name _____

1. _____

2. _____

3. _____

4. _____

5. _____

6. _____

7. _____

8. _____

9. _____

10. _____

Bakery Order Form

CAKES

Cake Flavor	Frosting Color
☐ chocolate	☐ blue
☐ vanilla	☐ green
☐ strawberry	☐ pink
	☐ yellow

Needed on: Monday   Tuesday   Wednesday   Thursday   Friday

Name _____

Bakery Order Form

PIES

☐ apple	☐ blueberry
☐ cherry	☐ lemon

Needed on: Monday   Tuesday   Wednesday   Thursday   Friday

Name _____

Bakery Order Form

MUFFINS

☐ banana   ☐ cinnamon

☐ blueberry   ☐ strawberry

Needed on: Monday   Tuesday   Wednesday   Thursday   Friday

Name _____

Bakery Order Form

COOKIES

☐ chocolate chip   ☐ oatmeal

☐ gingerbread   ☐ sugar

Needed on: Monday   Tuesday   Wednesday   Thursday   Friday

Name _____

Hair Salon, Barber Shop, Pet Store, Flower Shop, Book Store, or other store

Store Receipt		
Quantity	Item	Cost
	TOTAL	

References

Berk, Laura E., and Adam Winsler. 1995. *Scaffolding children's learning: Vygotsky and early childhood education*. Washington DC: National Association for the Education of Young Children.

Bodrova, Elena, and Deborah J. Leong. 2007. *Tools of the mind: The Vygotskian approach to early childhood education*. 2nd ed. Upper Saddle River, NJ: Pearson.

Boeree, George C. Abraham Maslow 1908–1970. http://www.ship.edu/~cgboeree (accessed May 25, 2009).

Bowman, Barbara. 2004. Play in the multicultural world of children: Implications for adults. In *Children's play: The roots of reading,* ed. Edward F. Zigler, Dorothy G. Singer, and Sandra J. Bishop-Josef, 125–42. Washington DC: Zero to Three Press.

Bredekamp, Sue. 2004. Play and school readiness. In *Children's play: The roots of reading,* ed. Edward F. Zigler, Dorothy G. Singer, and Sandra J. Bishop-Josef, 159–74. Washington DC: Zero to Three Press.

Carlsson-Paige, Nancy, and Diane E. Levin. 1990. *Who's calling the shots? How to respond effectively to children's fascination with war play and war toys*. Philadelphia, PA: New Society Publishers.

Copley, Juanita V. 2000. *The young child and mathematics*. Washington DC: National Association for the Education of Young Children.

Copple, Carol, and Sue Bredekamp, eds. 2009. *Developmentally appropriate practice in early childhood programs serving children from birth through age 8*. 3rd ed. Washington DC: National Association for the Education of Young Children.

Csikszentmihalyi, Mihaly. 1997. *Finding flow: The psychology of engagement with everyday life*. New York: Basic Books.

Curtis, Deb, and Margie Carter. 1996. *Reflecting children's lives: A handbook for planning child-centered curriculum.* St. Paul, MN: Redleaf Press.

————. 2003. *Designs for living and learning: Transforming early childhood environments.* St. Paul, MN: Redleaf Press.

Daniels, Ellen R., and Kay Stafford. 1999. *Creating inclusive classrooms.* Washington DC: Children's Resources International.

Derman-Sparks, Louise, and Julie Olsen Edwards. 2010. *Anti-bias education for young children and ourselves.* Washington DC: National Association for the Education of Young Children.

Dodge, Diane Trister, Laura J. Colker, and Cate Heroman. 2002. *The creative curriculum for preschool.* 4th ed. Washington DC: Teaching Strategies.

Gartrell, Dan. 2004. *The power of guidance: Teaching social-emotional skills in early childhood classrooms.* Clifton Park, NY: Thomson Delmar Learning.

Genishi, Celia, and Anne Haas Dyson. 2009. *Children, language, and literacy: Diverse learners in diverse times.* New York: Teachers College Press and Washington DC: National Association for the Education of Young Children.

Ginsburg, Kenneth R. 2007. The importance of play in promoting healthy child development and maintaining strong parent-child bonds. *Pediatrics* 119 (1): 182–91.

Gould, Patti, and Joyce Sullivan. 1999. *The inclusive early childhood classroom: Easy ways to adapt learning centers for all children.* Beltsville, MD: Gryphon House.

Gronlund, Gaye. 1992. Coping with Ninja Turtle play in my kindergarten classroom. *Young Children* 48 (1): 21–25.

————. 2003. *Focused early learning: A planning framework for teaching young children.* St. Paul, MN: Redleaf Press.

————. 2006. *Make early learning standards come alive: Connecting your practice and curriculum to state guidelines.* St. Paul, MN: Redleaf Press and Washington DC: National Association for the Education of Young Children.

Gronlund, Gaye, and Marlyn James. 2005. *Focused observations: How to observe children for assessment and curriculum planning.* St. Paul, MN: Redleaf Press.

————. 2008. *Early learning standards and staff development: Best practices in the face of change.* St. Paul, MN: Redleaf Press.

Hayes, Kathleen, and Reneé Creange. 2001. *Classroom routines that really work for preK and kindergarten.* New York: Scholastic.

Heidemann, Sandra, and Deborah Hewitt. 2010. *Play: The pathway from theory to practice.* St. Paul, MN: Redleaf Press.

Hendrick, Joanne, ed. 1997. *First steps toward teaching the Reggio way.* Upper Saddle River, NJ: Merrill.

Hestenes, Linda L., and Deborah E. Carroll. 2000. The play interactions of young children without disabilities: Individual and environmental influences. *Early Childhood Research Quarterly* 15 (2): 229–46.

Hoffman, Eric. 2004. *Magic capes, amazing powers: Transforming superhero play in the classroom.* St. Paul, MN: Redleaf Press.

Hutchins, Pat. 1986. *Rosie's walk.* New York: Aladdin Paperbacks.

Isenberg, Joan Packer, and Nancy Quisenberry. 2002. Play: Essential for all children. A position paper of the Association for Childhood Education International. http://www.acei.org/playpaper.htm.

Jacobs, Gera, and Kathy Crowley. 2007. *Play, projects, and preschool standards: Nurturing children's sense of wonder and joy in learning.* Thousand Oaks, CA: Corwin Press.

Johnson, James E., James F. Christie, and Francis Wardle. 2005. *Play, development, and early education.* Boston: Pearson.

Jones, Elizabeth, and Gretchen Reynolds. 1992. *The play's the thing: Teachers' roles in children's play.* New York: Teachers College Press.

Kagan, Sharon Lynn, and Amy E. Lowenstein. 2004. School readiness and children's play: Contemporary oxymoron or compatible option? In *Children's play: The roots of reading,* ed. Edward F. Zigler, Dorothy G. Singer, and Sandra J. Bishop-Josef, 59–76. Washington DC: Zero to Three Press.

Kantor, Rebecca, and Kimberlee L. Whaley. 1998. Existing frameworks and new ideas from our Reggio Emilia experience: Learning at a lab school with 2- to 4-year-old children. In *The hundred languages of children: The Reggio Emilia approach: Advanced reflections,* 2nd ed., ed. Carolyn Edwards, Lella Gandini, and George Forman, 313–34. Greenwich, CT: Ablex Publishing.

Katz, Lilian G., and Sylvia C. Chard. 1997. *Engaging children's minds: The project approach.* Greenwich, CT: Ablex Publishing.

Klein, Tovah P., Daniele Wirth, and Keri Linas. 2004. Play: Children's context for development. In *Spotlight on young children and play,* ed. Derry Gosselin Koralek, 28–35. Washington DC: National Association for the Education of Young Children.

Labinowicz, Ed. 1980. *The Piaget primer: Thinking, learning, teaching.* Menlo Park, CA: Addison-Wesley Publishing Company.

Maslow, Abraham H. 1970. *Motivation and personality.* New York: Harper and Row.

Medina, John. 2009. Keynote address delivered June 13 at the NAEYC Professional Development Institute in Charlotte, NC.

Miller, Edward, and Joan Almon. 2009. *Summary and recommendations of crisis in the kindergarten: Why children need to play in school.* College Park, MD: Alliance for Childhood.

The National Association for the Education of Young Children (NAEYC) and the National Association of Early Childhood Specialists (NAECS) in the State Departments of Education (SDE). 2002. Early learning standards: Creating the conditions for success. http://www.naeyc.org/about/positions/pdf/position_statement.pdf.

New, Rebecca S. 1998. Theory and praxis in Reggio Emilia: They know what they are doing, and why. In *The hundred languages of children: The Reggio Emilia approach: Advanced reflections*, 2nd ed., eds. Carolyn Edwards, Lella Gandini, and George Forman, 261–84. Greenwich, CT: Ablex Publishing.

Nimmo, John. 1998. The child in community: Constraints from the early childhood lore. In *The hundred languages of children: The Reggio Emilia approach: Advanced reflections*, 2nd ed., eds. Carolyn Edwards, Lella Gandini, and George Forman, 295–312. Greenwich, CT: Ablex Publishing.

Paley, Vivian Gussin. 1984. *Boys and girls: Superheroes in the doll corner*. Chicago: University of Chicago Press.

Pelo, Ann, and Fran Davidson. 2000. *That's not fair! A teacher's guide to activism with young children*. St. Paul, MN: Redleaf Press.

Roskos, Kathleen, and James Christie. 2004. Examining the play-literacy interface: A critical review and future directions. In *Children's play: The roots of reading*, ed. Edward F. Zigler, Dorothy G. Singer, and Sandra J. Bishop-Josef, 95–123. Washington DC: Zero to Three Press.

Saifer, Steffen. 2009. *Higher order play and its role in development and education*. Unpublished manuscript. Portland, OR: Northwest Regional Educational Laboratory.

Scieszka, Jon, and Lane Smith. 1996. *The true story of the three little pigs*. New York: Puffin Books.

Segal, Marilyn. 2004. The roots and fruits of pretending. In *Children's play: The roots of reading*, ed. Edward F. Zigler, Dorothy G. Singer, and Sandra J. Bishop-Josef, 33–48. Washington DC: Zero to Three Press.

Singer, Jerome L., and Mawiyah A. Lythcott. 2004. Fostering social achievement and creativity through sociodramatic play in the classroom. In *Children's play: The roots of reading*, ed. Edward F. Zigler, Dorothy G. Singer, and Sandra J. Bishop-Josef, 77–93. Washington DC: Zero to Three Press.

Vygotsky, L. 1976. Play and its role in the mental development of the child. In *Play: Its role in development and evolution*, ed. J. Bruner, A. Jolly, and K. Sylva, 537–54. New York: Basic Books.

Wenner, Melinda. 2009. The serious need for play. *Scientific American Mind*, February.

York, Stacey. 1998. *Big as life: The everyday inclusive curriculum*. 2 vols. St. Paul, MN: Redleaf Press.

Zigler, Edward F., and Sandra J. Bishop-Josef. 2004. Play under siege: A historical overview. In *Children's play: The roots of reading,* ed. Edward F. Zigler, Dorothy G. Singer, and Sandra J. Bishop-Josef, 1–14. Washington DC: Zero to Three Press.

Excerpt Credits

Excerpts from Bowman (2004) on pages 105 and 128 from Play in the multicultural world of children: Implications for adults by Barbara Bowman in *Children's play: The roots of reading* by Edward Zigler, Dorothy G. Singer, and Sandra J. Bishop-Josef, eds., 2004. Washington DC: Zero to Three Press.

Excerpt from Bredekamp (2004) on pages 17–18 from Play and school readiness by Sue Bredekamp in *Children's play: The roots of reading* by Edward Zigler, Dorothy G. Singer, and Sandra J. Bishop-Josef, eds., 2004. Washington DC: Zero to Three Press.

Excerpts from Copple and Bredekamp (2009) on pages 2, 4, 6, 29, 43, 53, 64, 66, 68–69, 74, 142, 152, and 157 from *Developmentally appropriate practice in early childhood programs serving children from birth through age 8,* 3rd ed. by Carol Copple and Sue Bredekamp, eds. Reprinted with permission from the National Association for the Education of Young Children.

Excerpts from Genishi and Dyson (2009) on pages 7, 24, 61, 99, 100, and 122 from *Children, language, and literacy: Diverse learners in diverse times* by Celia Genishi and Anne Haas Dyson, 2009. New York: Teachers College Press. Reprinted with permission from Teachers College Press. © 2009 by Teachers College Press, Columbia University. All rights reserved.

Excerpt from Gronlund (1992) on pages 109–111 reprinted from Coping with Ninja Turtle play in my kindergarten classroom by Gaye Gronlund in *Young Children* 48 (1): 21–25. Reprinted with permission from the National Association for the Education of Young Children.

Excerpt from Hestenes and Carroll (2000) on page 87 reprinted from The play interactions of young children without disabilities: Individual and environmental influences by Linda L. Hestenes and Deborah E. Carroll in *Early Childhood Research Quarterly* 15 (2): 229–46. Reprinted with permission from Elsevier.

Excerpt from Isenberg and Quisenberry (2002) on page 6 from Play: Essential for all children by Joan Packer Isenberg and Nancy Quisenberry. A position paper of the Association for Childhood Education International, 2002. Reprinted with permission from the authors and the Association for Childhood Education International, 17904 Georgia Avenue, Suite 215, Olney, MD. © 2002 by the Association.

Excerpts from Kagan and Lowenstein (2004) on page 124 from School readiness and children's play: Contemporary oxymoron or compatible option? by Sharon Lynn Kagan and Amy E. Lowenstein in *Children's play: The roots of reading* by Edward Zigler, Dorothy G. Singer, and Sandra J. Bishop-Josef, eds., 2004. Washington DC: Zero to Three Press.

Excerpts from Roskos and Christie (2004) on page 26 from Examining the play-literacy interface: A critical review and future directions by Kathleen Roskos and James Christie in *Children's play: The roots of reading* by Edward Zigler, Dorothy G. Singer, and Sandra J. Bishop-Josef, eds., 2004. Washington DC: Zero to Three Press.

Excerpts from Segal (2004) on pages 106–107 from The roots and fruits of pretending by Marilyn Segal in *Children's play: The roots of reading* by Edward Zigler, Dorothy G. Singer, and Sandra J. Bishop-Josef, eds., 2004. Washington DC: Zero to Three Press.

Illustration and Photo Credits

Illustrations on pages 137 and 172 through 181 courtesy of Todd Balthazor

Photos on pages 12, 27, 66, and 94 courtesy of Cathy Boldger

Photos on pages 32 (bottom right), 51, 91, and 116 courtesy of Gail M. Holtz

Photos on pages 16, 22, 30, 122, 123, 130 (right), 133, 139, and 162 courtesy of Laura Hummel

Photos on pages 125 (left) and 136 courtesy of Suzanne Jeffers

Photos on pages 8, 75, and 125 (right) courtesy of Joyce R. Kinney

Photos on pages 4, 9, 25, 35 (right), 48, and 55 courtesy of Laurie Tischler

The remaining photos are courtesy of the author